THE DEVILS

This powerful historical drama tells the story of a community of Ursuline nuns in seventeenth-century France believed to be possessed with devils. The local priest, Grandier, is accused of being responsible for this act of sorcery, through the plotting of his enemies. The play reaches a sombre climax as Grandier is humiliated and martyred.

19m 5f and many extras

THE HEREFORD PLAYS

General Editor: E. R. Wood

Maxwell Anderson
Winterset

Robert Ardrey
Thunder Rock

Robert Bolt
A Man for All Seasons
The Tiger and the
Horse

Harold Brighouse
Hobson's Choice

Coxe and Chapman
Billy Budd

Gordon Daviot
Dickon

Barry England
Conduct Unbecoming

J. E. Flecker
Hassan

Ruth and Augustus
Goetz
The Heiress

H. Granville-Barker
The Voysey Inheritance

(Ed.) E. Haddon
Three Dramatic
Legends

Willis Hall
The Long and the Short
and the Tall

Fritz Hochwälder
The Strong are Lonely

Henrik Ibsen
The Master Builder
An Enemy of the People

D. H. Lawrence
The Widowing of Mrs
Holroyd and *The*
Daughter-in-Law

Roger MacDougall
Escapade

Arthur Miller
The Crucible
Death of a Salesman
All My Sons

André Obey
Noah

J. B. Priestley
An Inspector Calls
Time and the Conways
When We are Married

James Saunders
Next Time I'll Sing to
You
A Scent of Flowers

R. C. Sherriff
Journey's End

J. M. Synge
The Playboy of the
Western World and
Riders to the Sea

Brandon Thomas
Charley's Aunt

Peter Ustinov
Romanoff and Juliet

John Whiting
Marching Song
Saint's Day
A Penny for a Song
The Devils

Oscar Wilde
The Importance of
Being Earnest

Tennessee Williams
The Glass Menagerie

John Whiting

The Devils

with an Introduction by
RONALD HAYMAN

**HEINEMANN EDUCATIONAL BOOKS LTD
LONDON**

Heinemann Educational Books Ltd

LONDON   EDINBURGH   MELBOURNE   AUCKLAND   TORONTO
HONG KONG   SINGAPORE   KUALA LUMPUR
IBADAN   NAIROBI   JOHANNESBURG
NEW DELHI

ISBN 0 435 22943 5

**All rights whatsoever in this play are fully protected
and application for permission to perform must be made
in advance to: A. D. Peters, 10 Buckingham Street,
Adelphi, London W.C.1**

Published by
Heinemann Educational Books Ltd
48 Charles Street, London W1X 8AH
Printed in Great Britain by
Morrison and Gibb Ltd
London and Edinburgh

CONTENTS

CONTENTS

INTRODUCTION

I N the spring of 1960 when he wrote *The Devils* John Whiting was forty-two and he had not written a full-length play since 1954. The six years in which he should have been at the prime of his creative life were spent largely writing for the cinema—' editing, doctoring, rewriting and advising on filmscripts,' as he put it himself in his self-disparaging way. His public career as a playwright had started in 1951 as auspiciously as a playwright's career can possibly start. He was still an unknown repertory actor when his comedy *A Penny for a Song* was bought by a leading theatrical management, which gave it a production on the grand scale—at the Haymarket Theatre directed by Peter Brook with a starry cast. Within a few months another of Whiting's plays, *Saint's Day*, which he had submitted for the Festival of Britain competition at the Arts Theatre, had been picked out of nearly a thousand entries to be one of three plays which would be staged so that the judges could base their final decision on an actual production. *Saint's Day* was awarded the first prize, but the critics hated it and the public stayed away, as they did from *A Penny for a Song*.

Whiting's next play, *Marching Song*, was almost equally unpopular and when the following play *The Gates of Summer* (written 1953–4) collapsed on its pre-London tour—partly because the leading actress was ill—he lost heart. After planning a novel he started to write it as a play but gave up half-way through. His next attempt at a play was also abortive and, but for Peter Hall, he might never have written for the theatre again.

In 1952, when Peter Hall was still an undergraduate, he directed a production of *Saint's Day* at Cambridge, followed by one of *A Penny for a Song* in the summer of 1953. In 1952 Aldous Huxley's book *The Devils of Loudon* came out and as soon as he read it Whiting felt he would like to make it into a film. In 1957, when Peter Hall was running the Arts

Theatre, he commissioned Whiting to write the one-act play *No Why*, but this was never staged until 1964. Meanwhile Peter Hall was appointed director of the company at the Shakespeare Memorial Theatre, which was about to become the Royal Shakespeare Company. When he wanted a new play for its first London season at the Aldwych, Whiting was the playwright he approached. Not wanting to depart too abruptly from the Stratford-on-Avon routine, he asked for a costume play with a large cast. *The Devils* is the result.

It is not difficult to see why Whiting had been so fascinated by Huxley's book, which retells the story of the Ursuline nuns in seventeenth-century Loudon who were believed to be possessed by devils. The local parson, Urbain Grandier, was burnt at the stake as being the sorcerer responsible for the diabolical manifestations, a death engineered by his enemies, whose plotting was well served by the convincing show the nuns were putting on. A good-looking young man whose vocation as a priest did not stop him from having love affairs, Grandier had one with the daughter of the public prosecutor, abandoning her when she became pregnant. He never had any contact at all with the nuns who were to destroy him, but after he turned down an invitation to become their spiritual director, they started dreaming about him and having ' visions '. Led on by their neurasthenic prioress, Sister Jeanne of the Angels, they became more and more hysterical, producing symptoms well calculated to be taken as proof of diabolical possession and to incriminate Grandier. The exorcists encouraged them and soon they were denouncing him as a magician. When Richelieu sided with his enemies, the predicament of the amorous priest became hopeless.

Aldous Huxley's book is more than a mere history of what happened. It is more like a long essay or a series of variations on historical themes. His three central characters are Sister Jeanne, Grandier and Jean-Joseph Surin, a Jesuit zealot who was eventually given the task of exorcising the Prioress and apparently succeeded, but at the cost of becoming possessed—or mentally unbalanced—himself.

Until his premature death, he was convinced of his own damnation. But he did not come to Loudun until after Grandier had been burnt and he does not figure in Whiting's play.

Huxley keeps interrupting his narrative to discuss general questions like witchcraft, the possibility that devils may really exist, the orthodox Christian attitude to them, the nature of the soul, methods of coercion, the treatment of the insane and the disparity between the private reality of the individual and his social persona. Comparing the seventeenth-century attitudes with the modern, Huxley takes a pessimistic pleasure in showing that the differences are smaller than they usually seem.

Above all he is concerned to show that the human mind is perpetually faced with the choice between unregeneracy and enlightenment, self-assertion and self-transcendence. It is partly because it raises the question of surrendering the self to non-human powers that he chooses the subject of possession. As early as 1931 he had been interested, at least figuratively, in the idea. ' A great man,' he wrote, ' differs from ordinary men by being, as it were, possessed by more than human spirits.' And he went on to describe the ' devils ' in Clemenceau, the French Prime Minister during part of the first world war. In *The Devils of Loudun* he explains the possession of the nuns as being an imitation of the daemonic in a downward escape from the self, while Surin was escaping upwards in high-minded madness, just as mystics escape in ' dying to self '.

Huxley is vague about what the *self* consists of and he also rather dislikes it, so he is slightly over-eager to diagnose cases of attempted escape from it. He writes as though the only choice is between trying to overcome the self completely or being ensnared by it into remaining one of the ' ordinary nice unregenerate people ' who are all so alike. The only way out of dull mediocrity is to strive towards communion with the ' divine ground ' in the human soul in order to attain ' one-pointedness of being '. He argues that ' an urge to self-transcendence is almost as widespread and at times almost as powerful as the urge to self-assertion '. The ' insulated self ' is a prison from which various escapes are possible. Saints and mystics have sometimes succeeded in escaping upwards into spirituality, achieving a 'union with the spirit which links the unknown to the known'. There are also downward and horizontal escapes 'into subhuman or merely human substitutes for Grace'. Horizontal transcendence is the most common: Huxley uses the phrase without much precision to mean 'identification with a cause wider than one's own immediate interest', and he includes business, marriage, hobbies and scientific research in the category. The downward escape routes include alcohol, drugs, mass-hysteria and sexual debauchery.

Although there is no exact counterpart to these psychological generalizations in Whiting's play, they have clearly influenced it. He had always been interested in what it was that raised a great man above the level of ordinary men: *Saint's Day* and *Marching Song* both go into this question. And in *The Devils* Grandier's spiritual progress can be seen —in fact must be seen—as a series of attempts to escape from what Huxley calls the insulated self. Grandier makes attempts in all three directions—downwards, horizontally and upwards. Nor are these attempts merely those of an isolated individual. In so far as he is a hero he is in some sense representative of the whole of humanity at the same time as being exceptional. It is interesting to see how often the word *man* figures in the dialogue, together with other lines that question just what a man is.

This is one of the points of the opening dialogue between Adam, the chemist, and Mannoury, the surgeon. What is left inside the head of the corpse now hanging on the municipal gallows? Grandier's first conversation is with the Sewerman, who represents the lowest elements in humanity. 'But I'm a man, sir,' he insists. 'A dirty sinful man.' Within a moment he is starting a sentence to Grandier by saying, 'If you were a man, sir, and not a priest . . .' And again, immediately, when they talk about the corpse on the gallows, Grandier says 'He was a man, a young man'. And 'Manhood led him into the power of the senses.'

Then, when the priest is seen in conversation with the young widow Ninon, the same questions of manhood and humanity crop up:

NINON: I saw you that day just as a man. What's the matter?
GRANDIER: I wish words like that could still hurt me.
NINON: I've never seen you as anything but a man. Do you
  want to be more?
GRANDIER: Of course. Or less.
NINON: But how can you be a man of God without being a man?

This last question goes to the root of what leads to Grandier's undoing. If a man is an animal with animal lusts
and human weaknesses, what can a priest do to negate his
own nature? Inevitably racked by guilt, Grandier—in the
first scene where we see him on his own—prays to be
forgiven for ' years heavy with pride and ambition, love of
women and love of self. Years scandalously marred by
adornment and luxury, time taken up with being that
nothing, a man.'

Just as the priest is unable to repress the man in himself,
the nun is unable to repress the woman. Grandier under-
stands this:

Secluded women. They give themselves to God, but something
remains which cries out to be given to Man.

When Jeanne announces her decision to invite him to
become director of the convent, she says it is God who has
put him into her thoughts. In fact, of course, it is his
reputation. When she receives his letter refusing the
invitation, she tears it up, presses it to her body and bursts
into laughter when she finds herself on the point of praying:

I was about to address myself to God in this matter. Habit.
Habit. No. It must be to Man.

The dreadful revenge she has on Grandier has little to do
with personal malice against him but proceeds directly
from her frustration as a woman. This is the downward
escape from the self.

Meanwhile Grandier's love affair with the daughter of
the Public Prosecutor is giving him hope of what Huxley
calls horizontal transcendence.

There is a way of salvation through each other. . . . Hope of
coming to God by way of a fellow being. Hope that the path
which taken alone in awful solitude is a way of despair, can be

enlightened by the love of a woman. I have come to believe that by this simple act of commital, which I have done with my heart, it may be possible to reach God by way of happiness.

Alone together in his church at night they go secretly through a marriage ritual, but it is later, when Philippe's pregnancy forces him to break with her, that we get the clearest statement of the euphoria that physical fulfilment can bring.

I thought—yes, solemnly I thought—the body can transcend its purpose. It can become a thing of such purity that it can be worshipped to the limits of imagination. Anything is allowed. All is right. And such perfection makes for an understanding of the hideous state of existence.

The dissatisfaction constantly expressed in the play with normal existence and with the normal self has a great affinity with Huxley's.

Where Whiting departs completely from Huxley's Grandier and from historical fact is in making the tension between his upward and downward drives produce a strong resultant drive towards self-destruction. This first becomes apparent in the middle of Act Two:

GRANDIER: All worldly things have a single purpose for a man of my kind. Politics, power, the senses, riches, pride and authority. I choose them with the same care that you, sir, select a weapon. But my intention is different. I need to turn them against myself.
D'ARMAGNAC: To bring about your end?
GRANDIER: Yes. I have a great need to be united with God. Living has drained the need for life from me. My exercise of the senses has flagged to total exhaustion. I am a dead man, compelled to live.

This is why he is glad when d'Armagnac and de Cerisay, the Governor of Loudun and the Chief Magistrate, who have so far protected him against his enemies, are defeated by Richelieu, who persuades the King to order the demolition of the city's fortifications. This will leave the Governor virtually powerless.

But the road to self-destruction is not a straight one. An experience with a dying man makes Grandier fall in love with life all over again, and here he comes very close to upward self-transcendence. His feeling of love for the dying man and a meeting with some children on the dusty walk back to Loudun give him a sense of joy so intense that he feels he is creating God.

> I created Him from the light and the air, from the dust of the road, from the sweat of my hands, from gold, from filth, from the memory of women's faces, from great rivers, from children, from the works of man, from the past, the present, the future and the unknown. I caused Him to be from fear and despair. I gathered in everything from this mighty act, all I have known, seen and experienced. My sin, my presumption, my vanity, my love, my hate, my lust. And last I gave myself and so made God. And He was magnificent. For He is in all these things.

The most important conversation Grandier has in Act Three is with a priest, an old and simple man, Father Ambrose, who comes to comfort him in the condemned cell. He is not a good priest:

> A peasant boy who clung to the love of God because he was too awkward to ask for the love of man. I'm not a good example, my son.

But he succeeds in comforting Grandier, advising him to die by the senses as he has lived by them.

> AMBROSE: Offer God pain, convulsion and disgust.
> GRANDIER: Yes. Give Him myself.
> AMBROSE: Let Him reveal Himself in the only way you can understand.
> GRANDIER: Yes! Yes!
> AMBROSE: It is all any of us can do. We live a little while and in that little while we sin. We go to Him as we can. All is forgiven.
> GRANDIER: Yes. I am His child. It is true. Let Him take me as I am. . . . I am a sinful man and I can be accepted. It is not nothing going to nothing. It is sin going to forgiveness. It is a human creature going to love.

Before he is tortured Grandier is humiliated—deprived of his magnificent canonical robes, then shorn of his fine curls, his moustache, even his eyebrows. But when Jeanne sees him for the first time, she still finds him beautiful.

During the torture he stolidly refuses to confess to being a sorcerer but confesses readily to what he calls his real sins:

> I have been a man, I have loved women. I have been proud.
> I have longed for power.

He may scarcely look like a man now but he has the courage to remain one to the end.

The experience of writing *The Devils* had a profound effect on Whiting's attitudes. He said in an interview* that working on it had given him a greater awareness of the reality of evil. ' We talk about love and hate, good and evil, as if they were poles apart, but in fact they're virtually the same thing and in a sense they work in the same way. I no longer believe in the old liberal humanist view that man is basically good. He is open to either good or evil. It is up to him which he chooses.'

In Whiting's earlier plays there had been a strong contrast between the consciously literary rhetoric of the big speeches and the colloquial language of more casual conversation, but in *The Devils* this contrast is more marked than ever before, the colloquial language sometimes becoming almost telegraphic.

> MANNOURY: Well, we have had a nice talk.
> ADAM: Have we got anywhere?
> MANNOURY: Somebody at the door.
> ADAM: Can't be.
> MANNOURY: Is.
>   (ADAM *opens the door.* LAUBARDEMONT *stands there.*)
> ADAM: No business. Shut.

The effect of having done so much writing for the cinema can be observed not only in the writing of individual speeches but in the structure. Many of the scenes are extremely short, shifting us quickly from one group of characters to another as Whiting cuts cross-sectionally through Loudun society, from the Governor to the Sewerman. The town comes vividly to life, and never more memorably than at the end, when the forces of evil have

---

* With Richard Findlater. Published in John Whiting: *The Art of the Dramatist.* Alan Ross, London Magazine Editions, 1970.

triumphed and a charnel-house atmosphere seems to have spread through the whole of local society. Adam and Mannoury talk like two concentration camp doctors about human fat rendered down by heat to the consistency of candle wax, while the Governor and the Chief Magistrate, who have been drinking to distract themselves, have seen an old woman with human remains in a basket.

This reminds us of a scene near the beginning: Adam and Mannoury meet Grandier in the street when they are carrying a bucket containing the head of the man from the gallows, which they have bought for ninepence. They are taking it to Adam's house to dissect. Mannoury has always titivated himself with the fancy that one day the divinity of man, enclosed in an infinitesimal bag, will rest upon the point of his knife. Reason, too, is seated in the head. In the last scene it is Grandier's remains in the basket, and the dissecting that the play has done may have revealed no secrets about the divinity of man or the functioning of reason, his godlike faculty, but it has created a multi-dimensional structure in which evil has been shown masquerading as religion. Downward escapes from the self have been made to look like obedience to duty.

In what sense is it a historical play? Certainly Whiting had a fine historical sense, as he had already shown in the comedy *A Penny for a Song*. In *The Devils* he recreates a piece of history very colourfully, presenting a large and varied cast of characters, each one of which belongs convincingly to his historical context. But in studying the interplay of sexual, social, political, economic and religious pressures on emotion and behaviour, in analysing this elaborate conspiracy of men and women to destroy a man who was more human than they were, Whiting, like Huxley, was to some extent using history as a stalking horse. And like Huxley he obviously believed that though the twentieth century offers different opportunities for us to indulge the lower sides of our natures, more sophisticated methods of destruction, humanity is still essentially the same as it was then. That is the real subject of the play.

CAST OF FIRST LONDON PERFORMANCE

The Devils received its first performance at the Aldwych on 20 February 1961.

MANNOURY	Ian Holm
ADAM	James Bree
LOUIS TRINCANT	P. G. Stephens
PHILLIPE TRINCANT	Diana Rigg
JEAN D'ARMAGNAC	Patrick Allen
GUILLAUME DE CERISAY	Peter Jeffrey
A SEWERMAN	Clive Swift
URBAIN GRANDIER	Richard Johnson
NINON	Yvonne Bonnamy
DE LA ROCHEPOZAY	Derek Godfrey
FATHER RANGIER	David Sumner
FATHER BARRÉ	Max Adrian
SISTER JEANNE OF THE ANGELS	Dorothy Tutin
SISTER CLAIRE	Stephanie Bidmead
SISTER LOUISE	Mavis Edwards
DE LAUBARDEMONT	Patrick Wymark
FATHER MIGNON	Donald Layne-Smith
SISTER GABRIELLE	Patsy Byrne
PRINCE HENRI DE CONDÉ	Derek Godfrey
RICHELIEU	John Cater
LOUIS XIII	Philip Voss
BONTEMPS	Stephen Thorne
FATHER AMBROSE	Roy Dotrice
A CLERK	John Cater

The play was directed by Peter Wood and designed by Sean Kenny.

CHARACTERS

MANNOURY a surgeon
ADAM a chemist
LOUIS TRINCANT the Public Prosecutor
PHILLIPE TRINCANT
JEAN D'ARMAGNAC the Governor of Loudun
A SEWERMAN
URBAIN GRANDIER the Vicar of St Peter's
    Church
GUILLAUME DE CERISAY the Chief Magistrate
NINON a widow
DE LA ROCHEPOZAY the Bishop of Poitiers
FATHER RANGIER
FATHER BARRÉ
SISTER JEANNE OF THE ANGELS the
    prioress of St Ursula's Convent
SISTER CLAIRE
SISTER LOUISE
DE LAUBARDEMONT the King's Special
    Commissioner to Loudun
FATHER MIGNON
SISTER GABRIELLE
PRINCE HENRI DE CONDÉ
RICHELIEU
LOUIS XIII King of France
BONTEMPS a gaoler
FATHER AMBROSE
A CLERK
Townspeople, People from the Country,
Capuchins, Carmelites, Jesuits, and Soldiers

*The action of this play takes place in and near the town of
Loudun, and briefly at Paris, between the years 1623 and
1634.*

I

The streets of Loudun. Day.

A corpse hangs from the municipal gallows. Nearby, a sewerman works in a shallow drain.

People are coming from Saint Peter's Church. ADAM, *a chemist, and* MANNOURY, *a surgeon, among others.*

MANNOURY: Shall we go together?

ADAM: By all means.

MANNOURY: Don't catch my sleeve. He spoke as if he were God.

ADAM: Grandier?

MANNOURY: Grandier.

ADAM: Very rousing to the spirit.

MANNOURY: You think so? Hm.

ADAM: So small a town is lucky to have such a caretaker of souls. Did I say that as if I meant it?

MANNOURY: No. There are things, my dear Adam.

ADAM: Things, Mannoury?

MANNOURY: Don't gape. Things said and things done.

ADAM: By the priest? Yes, I've heard.

MANNOURY: Then see.

NINON, *a young widow, has come from the church. She goes away along the street.*

ADAM: With my own eyes.

MANNOURY: I've attended her. Medically.

ADAM: Have you?

MANNOURY: It's not widowhood gives that contentment. That walk.

ADAM: It takes a visit.

MANNOURY: It does.

They have come beneath the gallows.

ADAM: Hoo, he dangles.

MANNOURY: What idiot is this?

ADAM: They put him up last night.

MANNOURY: Compelling sight. What resides, Adam?

ADAM: I don't understand you.

MANNOURY: What's left, man? After that.

ADAM: Ah, you've something in your head.

MANNOURY: Has he? That's the point. Come to dinner.

ADAM *and* MANNOURY *go.*

LOUIS TRINCANT *and his daughter,* PHILLIPE, *have come from the church.*

TRINCANT: Fold your hands, child. You walk like a peasant.

PHILLIPE: Who's to see?

TRINCANT: The world. Let it set eyes on a lady.

They have come near the gallows.

PHILLIPE: Was he young or old?

TRINCANT: Don't look.

PHILLIPE: You want me to be filled with nice and useful experience, Father, so tell me something: does death unmask the face in heaven?

TRINCANT: A question for a priest.

PHILLIPE: I'm sorry. Let's talk of how my legs move in the dance. And of marriage. And love. Not death. For death smells bad. And there is scent upon a pillow.

TRINCANT: Chatter. Come along. Mind the step.

TRINCANT *and* PHILLIPE *go*.

JEAN D'ARMAGNAC, *Governor of the town, and* GUILLAUME DE CERISAY, *the Chief Magistrate, have come from the church into the street.*

D'ARMAGNAC: Grandier seems to have got it into his head that the forces of good are a kind of political party, needing a leader.

DE CERISAY: His mind's been running on such things.

D'ARMAGNAC: Politics? All the same, the terms seem strange coming from a pulpit.

DE CERISAY: So does wit.

D'ARMAGNAC: Yes. I disgraced myself this morning. I laughed aloud. Is that more becoming to the Governor of the town than yawning his way through the sermon, as I used to do before Grandier came here?

DE CERISAY: Have you sent the carriage on?

D'ARMAGNAC: Yes, I thought we'd walk. Tell me—

DE CERISAY: Yes?

D'ARMAGNAC: This is a small town. Can it contain a Father Grandier? That proud man. Shall we go this way?

D'ARMAGNAC *and* DE CERISAY *go.*

The crowd has gone. The church doorway is empty.

FATHER URBAIN GRANDIER, *Vicar of Saint Peter's Church, appears. He comes into the street. A bucket of filth dredged up by the sewerman splashes his gown.*

SEWERMAN: Sorry.

GRANDIER: It doesn't matter.

SEWERMAN: It's wrong, though. Shit on the holy purple.

GRANDIER: My son—

SEWERMAN: Father?

GRANDIER: Your words suit your condition.

SEWERMAN: How would you have it?

GRANDIER: Otherwise.

SEWERMAN: But I'm a man, sir. A dirty, sinful man. And my job is in the drains of the city. Why expect clean words from me? Let me oblige you, all the same. I regret, sir, splashing your gown with the excrement of the poor. Better?

GRANDIER (*he laughs*): It'll do.

SEWERMAN: Lovely day. Hot.

GRANDIER: Yes. How can you bear to work down there?

SEWERMAN: Well, I used to keep my mind on higher things.

GRANDIER: I'm very pleased to hear it. What were they?

SEWERMAN: My wife and my dinner.

GRANDIER: I see. But now—

SEWERMAN: There's not the need. I've grown used to the stink. Nobody can live forty-three years and not have it happen. If you were a man, sir, and not a priest, perhaps I could make you understand.

GRANDIER: Try, even so.

SEWERMAN: Well, every man is his own drain. He carries his main sewer with him. Gutters run about him to carry off the dirt—

GRANDIER: They also carry the blood of life.

SEWERMAN: Mere plumbing. Elementary sanitation. Don't interrupt. And what makes a man happy? To eat, and set the drains awash. To sit in the sun and ferment the rubbish. To go home, and find comfort in his wife's conduit. Then why should I feel ashamed or out of place down here?

GRANDIER: Put in that way I can see no reason at all. It must be almost a pleasure.

SEWERMAN: It's clear, sir, that your precious juices will never flow here. As this misguided creature has dripped through his toes all night.

GRANDIER: Don't mock the thing!

SEWERMAN: Sorry.

GRANDIER: He was a man. A young man. Eighteen years old. They brought him to kneel at the church door on his way here. He told me his sins.

SEWERMAN: What were they?

GRANDIER: Being alive.

SEWERMAN: Comprehensive.

GRANDIER: Heinous, it seemed. Manhood led him into the power of the senses. With them he worshipped in total adoration a young girl. But he learnt too quickly. He learnt that only gold can decorate the naked body. And so he stole.

SEWERMAN: And so he hanged.

GRANDIER: He confessed something to me alone. It was not for God to hear. It was a man speaking to a man. He said that when he adorned the girl the metal looked colourless, valueless, against her golden skin. That was repentance. When will they take him down?

SEWERMAN: Tomorrow. When it's dark.

GRANDIER: See that it's done with some kind of decency.

GRANDIER *goes.*

DE CERISAY: D'ARMAGNAC: TRINCANT.

D'ARMAGNAC: Provincial life, my dear Trincant.

TRINCANT: You feel it has a bad effect on the art of poetry?

D'ARMAGNAC: Ask De Cerisay.

DE CERISAY: Well, you and I, Trincant, as Public Prosecutor and Magistrate, are brought close to the ground by our work. I've always understood poetry to be an elevated art.

TRINCANT: I assure you that during composition I think the right thoughts. My mind, if I may put it this way, is filled with nobility.

DE CERISAY: Why don't you show this latest bunch of Latin epigrams to Grandier?

TRINCANT: The priest?

DE CERISAY: As a priest his secular senses are well developed. Make a selection. Submit them. The man is a scholar.

TRINCANT: Very well. I don't seek praise, but I'll do as you say. Yes.

TRINCANT *goes.*

D'ARMAGNAC: Poor Trincant. He loves the Muses but, alas, they don't seem to love him. I hope your suggestion about Grandier was not malicious.

DE CERISAY: Not at all, sir, As with any author, the greater Trincant's audience the less burden of doubt on his closer friends.

D'ARMAGNAC: Grandier came to see me this morning. I was having breakfast in the garden. He didn't know that I could observe him as he walked towards me. Vulnerable: smiling. He visibly breathed the air. He stopped to watch the peacocks. He fondled a rose as if it were the secret part of a woman. He laughed with the gardener's child. Then he composed himself, and it was another man who sat down beside me and talked for an hour. Where will this other man climb on his ladder of doubt and laughter?

DE CERISAY: Probably to the highest offices of the church.

D'ARMAGNAC: And the man I saw in the garden?

Silence.

GRANDIER *with* NINON.   *A disordered bed: biretta on the bedpost.*

NINON: Tell me.

GRANDIER: Now what do you need to be told?   Words are playthings in our situation. Expect music from them, but not sense.

NINON: Don't laugh at me. I never understand. I'm not a clever woman.

GRANDIER: You're too humble, Ninon. It's a female vice. It will never do. Ask your question.

NINON: Why do you come to me?

GRANDIER: That would be a wise question if we were in your drawing room. As it is—

NINON: There are pretty young girls in the town.

GRANDIER: They didn't need consolation for the untimely death of their husband, the rich wine merchant. That was the reason for my first visit, remember. How many Tuesdays ago was it? I asked you to believe that God loved you, and had you in His eternal care. That the bursting of your husband's heart at the dinner table, when his blood ran with his wholesale wine, was an act of love. That all things, however incomprehensible, are an act of love. But you couldn't bring yourself to believe any of this. Your soul is as tiny as your mind, Ninon, and you had to fall back on a most human gesture: you wept. Tears must be wiped away. How can that be done without a caress?

NINON: I saw you that day just as a man. What's the matter?

GRANDIER: I wish words like that could still hurt me.

He is putting scent on his handkerchief.

NINON: I've never seen you as anything but a man. Do you want to be more?

GRANDIER: Of course. Or less.

NINON: But how can you be a man of God without being a man?

GRANDIER: My dear child, you ask questions out of your time, and far beyond your experience. Your mouth . . .

A bell is sounding.

NINON: You possess me.

GRANDIER: Go to sleep now. You've been a good little animal today. Let the thought of it comfort you. Be happy.

GRANDIER *goes.*

ADAM *and* MANNOURY: *a table between them.*

MANNOURY: This human head fills me with anticipation, my dear Adam.

ADAM: It's a common enough object.

MANNOURY: Every man wears one on his shoulders, certainly. But when a head comes into my hands dis-associated from the grosser parts of the body I always feel an elevation of spirit. Think, this is the residence of reason.

ADAM: Indeed! Ah, yes. Very true.

MANNOURY: Isn't it possible that one day in the most commonplace dissection I might find —

ADAM: What Mannoury? Don't hesitate to tell me.

MANNOURY: I might stumble upon the very meaning of reason. Isn't it possible that the divinity of man, enclosed in an infinitesimal bag, might rest upon the point of my knife? I have dreamed of the moment. I have seen myself. I lift the particle, taken from the cerebellum and, Adam, I know!

ADAM: What do you know, Mannoury?

MANNOURY: Come, my dear friend, I am speaking in the most comprehensive sense. I know—everything. All—is revealed.

ADAM: God bless my soul!

MANNOURY: Let's take this thing to your house. We'll spend the evening on it.

They begin to go down into the street.

MANNOURY: Everyone is speaking of your treatment of the Duke's love disease.

ADAM: Yes, I think we're getting on top of it. Too soon to be certain.

MANNOURY: Your metallic compound. Does it affect the potency?

ADAM: Disastrously. But as I jokingly told the Duke, Science must concern itself with primary causes. It cannot turn its head to observe destructive side issues.

MANNOURY: And never will, we must hope.

ADAM: Is Madam Who Shall Be Nameless delivered?

MANNOURY: Prematurely. The fœtus was interesting. It had a tiny cap drawn over its head.

ADAM: Hardly surprising with all this talk about the coachman.

They are now in the street. GRANDIER *is approaching them.*

MANNOURY: Look who's coming.

ADAM: Studied indifference, if you please.

GRANDIER: Good evening, Mister Surgeon. And Mister Chemist.

MANNOURY: Good evening, sir.

ADAM: Sir.

GRANDIER: It's been a fine day.

MANNOURY: Yes.

ADAM: It has.

GRANDIER: But now—rain, do you think?

ADAM: The sky is clear.

MANNOURY: It is.

GRANDIER: But it may cloud before night.

ADAM: Indeed.

MANNOURY: Indeed, it may.

GRANDIER: Darken, you know. What have you got in that bucket?

MANNOURY: A man's head.

GRANDIER: A friend?

MANNOURY: A criminal.

ADAM: The body was taken down from the gallows last night.

GRANDIER (*after silence*): I hope they didn't overcharge you, in the interest of Science.

MANNOURY: Ninepence.

GRANDIER: Reasonable. A bargain. Let me see. Poor pickle.

ADAM: Yes. Mannoury and I have been discussing the human predicament with this relic as centrepiece.

GRANDIER: I'm sure you said some very interesting things.

ADAM: Well, Mannoury did observe that the seat of reason is situated here.

GRANDIER: How true! But you'll have said that, Adam.

ADAM: I did.

GRANDIER: And we mustn't forget looking down on this pudding that man's fiddledeevinity is what you may say only to the greater purpose of his hohumha.

ADAM: I beg your pardon.

GRANDIER: I quite agree. But I mustn't stay exchanging profundities with you, however much you may tempt me. So goodbye, Mister Surgeon and Mister Chemist.

GRANDIER *goes. The bell is sounding.*

MANNOURY: You fell into his trap, Adam. Never engage Mister Clever.

ADAM: He smelled of the widow woman. Filth.

MANNOURY: Of course. He's just come from her.

ADAM: After tickling himself in the confessional with the sins of young girls this morning—

MANNOURY: He consummates himself in the widow's bed this afternoon—

ADAM: And then comes and yawns in our faces.

MANNOURY: Tonight—

ADAM: Tonight he'll spend in some great house. D'Armagnac's, De Cerisay's. Fed, comforted, and flattered by the laughter of women.

MANNOURY: What a—I'm so sorry. What were you going to say?

ADAM: I was going to say, What a life!

MANNOURY: So was I.

ADAM: We're never asked to such places.

MANNOURY: I've thought of it often.

ADAM: How do you console yourself?

MANNOURY: By remembering that I'm an honest man doing an honest job.

ADAM: Is that enough?

MANNOURY: What do you mean?

ADAM: Pick up the head and come with me.

They go along the street and into a house.

GRANDIER *enters the church. He kneels at the altar: prays.*

GRANDIER: O my dear Father, it is the wish of Your humble child to come to Your Grace. I speak in the weariness of thirty-five years. Years heavy with pride and ambition, love of women and love of self. Years scandalously marred by adornment and luxury, time taken up with being that nothing, a man.

I prostrate myself before You now in ravaged humility of spirit. I ask You to look upon me with love. I beg that You will answer my prayer. Show me a way. Or let a way be made.

Silence.

O God, O my God, my God! Release me. Free me. These needs! Have mercy. Free me. Four o'clock of a Tuesday afternoon. Free me.

He rises: cries out.

Rex tremendae majestatis, qui salvandos salvas gratis, salva me, salva me, fons pietatis!

DE LA ROCHEPOZAY, *Bishop of Poitiers: Capuchins and Carmelites.*

DE LA ROCHEPOZAY: I have been alone for many days now. You will want to know if I have found some kind of grace. Perhaps, for I am filled with weariness and disgust at the folly and wickedness of mankind. Is this the beneficence of God, you ask? It may well be. Let me tell you the circumstances of the revelation.

Shut in my room for seven days, fasting and at prayer, I came to see myself as the humble instrument of God's will. It was a state of such happiness, such bliss and such abasement that I wished never to return to you. I longed for this husk to wither away, leaving only the purity of spirit. But my sense of duty as your bishop forced me to leave this paradise. I came back to the world.

A priest of Loudun, called Grandier, wished to see me. He is my child, as you all are, my darling, and I would wish to love him. But his handkerchief was scented.

If this man had struck me in the face it would have

humiliated me less. The assault on my senses was so obscene that I was in a state of terror. Scent, for a man to whom the taste of water was like fire, and the sound of the birds in the garden like the screams of the damned.

I am very tired. Take these rings from my fingers.

Perhaps on your way here from your parish a child smiled at you, or you were attracted by a flower, or the smell of new grass by the road. Did you think of these things with anything but pleasure? One of you may have lost your way and been directed by a stranger. Did you think of it as anything but kindness?

Let me say this to you. There is no innocence, none! Suspect goodness in men, and reject kindness.

For all vanities are an assertion of self, and the assertion of self in Man is the ascendancy of the Devil.

When that handkerchief was flourished in my face this morning I saw it as if in a vision. It became a mighty banner flung across the world, stinking, enveloping, overwhelming our beloved Church in shamelessness and lust. We are in peril!

Take me away. Take me away.

DE LA ROCHEPOZAY *is led away.* FATHER BARRÉ *and* FATHER RANGIER *are left alone.*

RANGIER: How are things in your part of the world?

BARRÉ: I'm kept very busy.

RANGIER: Is he among you?

BARRÉ: Incessantly.

RANGIER: Can we name him?

BARRÉ: If you want to. Satan.

RANGIER: How is the struggle?

BARRÉ: I shan't give up.

RANGIER: You look tired.

BARRÉ: It goes on day and night.

RANGIER: Your spirit is shining

BARRÉ: Unbroken, at any rate.   But there's never a moment's peace at Chinon now.   Only the other day I was conducting a marriage.   Everything was going very well.   I had before me a young couple, ignorant, I thought, but pure.   It never entered my head that they were anything else.   I'd reached the blessing, and was about to send them out to the world as man and wife, when there was a disturbance at the west door.   A cow had come into the church, and was trying to force its way through the congregation.   I knew at once, of course.

RANGIER: That it was he?

BARRÉ: Say it, Rangier, say it.   (*He shouts*) It was Satan!

RANGIER: You're never taken in.

BARRÉ: Before I could act he had passed from the cow to the bride's mother, who fell to the ground in a kind of convulsion.   There was the most dreadful confusion, of course, but I began exorcism at once.   There's a couple that won't forget their wedding day in a hurry.

RANGIER: How did it end?

BARRÉ: The spirit screamed from the church like a great wind.   A kind of black slime was found smeared on the girl's forehead.   She said she'd fallen, but of course I know better.   That's not all.   Two days later the husband came to me and said he'd found himself quite unable to perform his necessary duty.   The usual kind of spell, you know. I've now started investigations into the whole family.

RANGIER: This sort of thing must bring a lot of people to Chinon.

BARRÉ: Thousands.

RANGIER: There's great popular interest in evil nowadays.

BARRÉ: It's certainly helped to offset the sadly declining attendance at my shrine. The image of Notre-Dame de Recouvrance.

RANGIER: Well, you know how that's come about.

BARRÉ: Certainly. They all flock to Loudun now. This Grandier person, who's upset the bishop, is responsible for that. He touts for his place disgracefully.

RANGIER: There are fashions in miracle working images, just as there are in women's hats.

BARRÉ: That's true. But there's a satisfying constancy in evil. I must go.

RANGIER: Anything interesting?

BARRÉ: I have to call at a farm. They say that something is speaking through the umbilicus of a child. The child herself is now in conversation with it, and I'm told the two voices have evolved a quite astonishing creed of profanation.

BARRÉ *and* RANGIER *go separate ways.*

GRANDIER *alone. He has a sheaf of poems in his hand.* TRINCANT *comes to him.*

TRINCANT: So good of you to call, Father Grandier.

GRANDIER: Not at all. I've brought back your poetry.

TRINCANT: So I see. D'Armagnac holds that any insufficiency must be put down to life in the provinces.

GRANDIER: You write them when you get back from the office.

TRINCANT: Every day.

GRANDIER: Amid the cooking smells.

TRINCANT: They drift up.

GRANDIER: And the clatter of family life.

TRINCANT: It intrudes.

GRANDIER: And so naturally you achieve—these.

TRINCANT: Put me out of my misery. I want an honest opinion.

GRANDIER: You're an important man in this town, Trincant. Men in public positions can't expect honesty.

TRINCANT: Speak to me as a poet, not as Public Prosecutor.

GRANDIER: Very well. Your poetry—

PHILLIPE TRINCANT *has come in.*

TRINCANT: What is it?

PHILLIPE: I want my sewing, Father.

TRINCANT: Please take it. (*To Grandier*) This is my elder daughter, Phillipe. What were you saying?

GRANDIER: I was about to say that your creations—these—have great merit. They seem to be moral observations of a most uncommon kind.

TRINCANT: Really?

GRANDIER: *(to Phillipe)*: Don't you think so? I'm speaking of your father's poetry.

TRINCANT: She's very ignorant about such things. Young girls, you know, dear me. Dancing, music and laughter. Finer things can go hang.

GRANDIER: She should be instructed.

TRINCANT: It's so difficult to find anyone suitable in this town. Unless—

GRANDIER *(to Phillipe)*: Do you speak any Latin?

PHILLIPE: A little.

GRANDIER: That's not enough.

TRINCANT: Unless—

GRANDIER: It's an exact language. Makes it possible to say just what you mean. That's rare nowadays. Don't you agree?

PHILLIPE: Yes, it is.

TRINCANT: Unless you, Father Grandier, would undertake the instruction.

GRANDIER: Of your daughter?

TRINCANT: Yes.

GRANDIER: I'm a busy man.

TRINCANT: Just one day a week. A few hours in the appreciation of finer things. It could be done by conversation. Perhaps the reading of suitable Latin verse.

GRANDIER: Very well.

TRINCANT: Shall we say Tuesday?

GRANDIER: No. Not Tuesday. The next day.

ADAM *and* MANNOURY: *they sit in the pharmacy, beneath a stuffed crocodile and hanging bladders. Light is reflected through bottles which hold malformed creatures.*

ADAM (*he is reading from a small book*): At half-past five on Tuesday he left the widow's house.

MANNOURY: The man is a machine. Interesting, though. Can sexual response be conditioned by the clock?

ADAM: At half-past seven he was observed in public conversation with D'Armagnac. The subject is in doubt, although Grandier was seen to snigger twice. He dined alone, later than usual, at nine o'clock. A light burned in his room until after midnight.

MANNOURY: I suppose it's possible. I say to a woman: At four-thirty on Tuesday I shall arrive to pleasure you. I do so on the dot for some weeks. It no longer becomes necessary to say that I shall do so. Anticipation speaks for me. Tuesday: half-past four. Usual physiological manifestations. Subject for treatise. Must think.

ADAM (*he turns a page*): Discovered at dawn prostrate before altar. Great languor through the morning. A meal at a quarter past two. Sweetbreads in cream, followed by a rank cheese. Wine. Three o'clock: entered Trincant's house for instruction of Trincant's daughter, Phillipe.

MANNOURY: Adam, you're a wit.

ADAM: Am I, now?

MANNOURY: Your inflexion on the word 'instruction' was masterly.

ADAM: Thank you.

MANNOURY: But forgive me, my dear friend, if I ask you something. How do we go on? Your observations of Grandier's movements are a marvel. But these are the habits of any man. We shall never catch him on such evidence.

ADAM: You must give me time, Mannoury. We shall never expose him on his habits, certainly. But lust is leading him by the nose. And lust must have a partner. The widow, Ninon? Phillipe Trincant? Another? Who knows? But there will be a time. Patience.

SISTER JEANNE-DES-ANGES *alone: kneeling.*

JEANNE: I dedicate myself humbly to Your service. You have made me, both in stature and in spirit, a little woman. And I have a small imagination, too. That is why, in Your infinite wisdom, You have given me this visible burden on my back to remind me day by day of what I must carry. O my dear Lord, I find it difficult to turn in my bed, and so in the small and desperate hours I am reminded of Your burden, the Cross, on the long road.

You have brought meaning to my life by my appointment to this Ursuline house. I will try to guide the Sisters of this place. I will do my duty as I see it. (*silence*) Lord . . . Lord, I have had great difficulty with prayer ever since I was a little girl. I have longed for another and greater voice within me to praise you. By Your grace I have come young to this office. Have mercy on Your child. Let her aspire. Meanwhile, the floors shall be swept, the beds neatly made, and the pots kept clean.

(*Silence*) Mercy. (*silence*) I will find a way. Yes, I will find a way to You. I shall come. You will enfold me in Your sacred arms. The blood will flow between us, uniting us. My innocence is Yours.

(Silence: precisely) Please God, take away my hump so that I can lie on my back without lolling my head. *(silence)* There is a way to be found. May the light of Your eternal love . . . *(whispers)*.

Amen

SISTER JEANNE *rises: goes.*

GRANDIER *and* PHILLIPE: *she is reading.*

PHILLIPE: Foeda est in coitu et brevis voluptas, et taedet Veneris statis peractae.

GRANDIER: Translate as you go. Line by line.

PHILLIPE: Pleasure in love is . . .

GRANDIER: Lust.

PHILLIPE: Pleasure in lust is nasty and short, And sickness . . .

GRANDIER: Weariness.

PHILLIPE: And weariness follows on desire.

GRANDIER: Go on.

PHILLIPE: non ergo ut pecudes libidinosae caeci protinus irruamus illuc (nam languescit amor peritque flamma); *(pause)*
We're not like animals to rush at it,
Love dies there, and the flame goes out.

GRANDIER: Prosaic, but fair. Give me the book. *(he translates)*

But in everlasting leisure,
Like this, like this, lie still
And kiss time away.
No weariness and no shame,
Now, then and shall be all pleasure.
No end to it,
But an eternal beginning.

My child, why are you crying?

PHILLIPE: I haven't been well.

GRANDIER: Do you find our little lessons too much for you?

PHILLIPE: No, no, I love—I enjoy them very much.

GRANDIER: Well, we've only had six. I thought they might go on say to the end of the year.

PHILLIPE: Of course. As long as you like.

GRANDIER: As long as *you* like, Phillipe. They're for your benefit.

PHILLIPE: I want very much to understand. All things.

GRANDIER: All things?

PHILLIPE: There are forces inside me as a woman which must be understood if they are to be resisted.

GRANDIER: What forces, Phillipe?

PHILLIPE: Inclinations—

GRANDIER: Go on.

PHILLIPE: Inclinations towards sin.

Silence.

D'ARMAGNAC *stands at a high point on the fortifications of the town.*

A Council of State.   Distant figures: LOUIS XIII, *King of France, and* RICHELIEU.

RICHELIEU: It is a simple matter to understand sir.   You have that paper upside down.   The self-government of the small provincial towns of France must be brought to an end.   The first step is to pull down all kinds of fortification.

GRANDIER *has approached D'Armagnac from below.*

D'ARMAGNAC: So it's the turn of this city.

GRANDIER: Is everything to come down?

D'ARMAGNAC: That's what they want.   It's a trick, of course.   Richelieu sits with the King in Paris.   He whispers in his ear.

RICHELIEU: France must be free within herself if she is to determine her own destiny.

D'ARMAGNAC: Ignorant and crafty provincials like us cannot see beyond the city walls.   So we have this order from the Cardinal to tear them down.   Will it broaden our view?

RICHELIEU: Such men as your friend D'Armagnac, sir, see with little vision.   Their loyalty is to their town, not to France.

GRANDIER: Have they given any reason for this order?

D'ARMAGNAC: When a man's intent on power, as Richelieu is, he can justify his actions with absurdities.

RICHELIEU: Such fortifications provide opportunities for an uprising by the Protestants.

D'ARMAGNAC: Look. An old city. Those walls keep out more than the draught. Those towers are more than ornament. And from that fortress I have tried to administer my small sovereignty with reasonable wisdom. For I love the place.

GRANDIER: You must refuse to destroy it. Will other provincial governors stand against the order?

D'ARMAGNAC: It's very doubtful.

GRANDIER: Shall we?

D'ARMAGNAC: We?

GRANDIER: Let me help you in this matter, sir.

D'ARMAGNAC: Do you mean it? There is a churchman beside the King in Paris. As another, beside me here, do you also want to use this matter for your own ends?

GRANDIER: Conflict attracts me, sir. Resistance compels me.

D'ARMAGNAC: They can destroy you.

GRANDIER: I am weak, it's true. But equal power cannot be conflict. It is negation. Peace. So let me help you with all the passion of my failure.

D'ARMAGNAC: Don't smile. They can destroy you.

DE LAUBARDEMONT, *the King's Commissioner, has come to stand below Richelieu and the King.* RICHELIEU *speaks to him.*

RICHELIEU: D'Armagnac, the Governor of Loudun, has refused to obey the order. Go to the town. You've served me before. Wait. There is a man. His name is Grandier. He is a priest. Yes, there is a man called Grandier. Remember that.

DE LAUBARDEMONT *goes.*

An unseen woman's voice:

> Lux aeterna luceat eis, Domine, cum sanctis tuis in aeternum, quia pius est.
>
> Requiem aeternam dona eis, Domine, et lux perpetua luceat eis.

SISTER JEANNE DES ANGES: SISTER CLAIRE OF ST JOHN: SISTER LOUISE OF JESUS: SISTER GABRIELLE OF THE INCARNATION: *they enter.*

JEANNE: We have suffered a great loss, Sisters. Canon Moussaut was a good old man.

CLAIRE: It is God's will.

LOUISE: God's will.

JEANNE: So we have been taught. All the same, his death leaves us with a problem. We lack a director. The old man served this place well for many years, it's true, but the life of sinful children must go on. Penitents, we must have a confessor.

LOUISE: Have you chosen, Mother?

JEANNE: God will choose.

CLAIRE: We will pray.

JEANNE: Do so. There is a—(*fit of coughing*) Don't touch my back! (*stillness: exhaustion*) There is a man. His name is Grandier. He is young. I have never seen him, but God has often put him in my thoughts lately. I mean to . . . (*silence*).

CLAIRE: What's the matter?

JEANNE: Claire?

CLAIRE: Why stare at me like that? Have I done something wrong?

JEANNE (*seeing the girl*): No, no. I mean to write to this good man and invite him to be our new director. Grandier. Grandier. It is guidance, you understand. He has been put in my thoughts. Grandier.

CLAIRE: It is God's will.

LOUISE: God's will.

JEANNE (*sudden harsh laughter*): I am tired to death. (*silence: calmly*) It is a very excellent and practical solution. He can advise us on the method of education for the children put in our care. He will oversee our spiritual needs. (*laughter again*) He can sort out these damned problems of theological progression which muddle me day after day. Yes, it will be a good appointment. Leave me alone.

The Sisters go: JEANNE *calls back* CLAIRE.

JEANNE: Claire!

CLAIRE: Yes?

JEANNE: They say I have beautiful eyes. Is it true?

CLAIRE: Yes, Mother.

JEANNE: Too beautiful to close even in sleep, it seems. Go with the others.

JEANNE *alone.*

JEANNE: A summer morning. Children playing. Boy and girl. Paper boats sail the pond. Sun shone so hot upon the head that day. Children crouched, staring at each other across the sheet of water. Was it love? Flick. A toad upon a slab. Croak. Boy, head to one side, smiling, gentle voice whispering over the water: Look. Speak to

your brother, Jeanne. There. Green brother. Hophop.
Speak to him, Jeanne. (*laughter: silence*) God, forgive
my laughter. But you haven't given me much defence,
have You?

JEANNE *goes to a window and opens it. She stares down through
the grille upon:*

*A street. There is a market stall. People of the town are
coming and going, buying and selling. Children. A cart passes.
A song is heard.*

GRANDIER *comes through the crowd. He is in full canonicals, magnificent, golden, in the dying light of day. His tread
is quick, confident and gay.*

JEANNE *cries out.*

The sound is not heard by the crowd, but GRANDIER *stops.
He looks around him, into the faces of the crowd, wondering
which man or woman could have been moved to such a cry of
agony in the middle of such careless activity.* GRANDIER
goes on by way of ascending steps.

JEANNE *is writing. Rapid, angular hand, ornamented.*

The street. ADAM *and* MANNOURY *are among the crowd. They
come forward.*

MANNOURY: The first thing to do is to draw up some kind
of document.

ADAM: An accusation against Grandier.

MANNOURY: Exactly. We know about his debauchery.

ADAM: Profanity.

MANNOURY: And impiety.

ADAM: Is it enough?

MANNOURY: It'll have to do.

ADAM: For the time being.

MANNOURY: We'll present the paper to the Bishop.

ADAM: It must be properly done.

MANNOURY: Of course. Framed in correct language, decent to handle—

ADAM: Something's just occurred to me.

MANNOURY: Oh?

ADAM: What a lot of criticism we middle classes come in for just because we like things nice. I'm sorry. Go on. What will the document say?

MANNOURY: Say? (*pause*) We shall have to decide.

ADAM: It's not important.

MANNOURY: No. Just the means.

ADAM: We must keep the end in sight.

MANNOURY: Always.

They go.

A confessional: GRANDIER *and* PHILLIPE. *They speak in whispers throughout.*

GRANDIER: When was your last confession, child?

PHILLIPE: A week ago, Father.

GRANDIER: What have you to tell me?

PHILLIPE: Father, I have sinned. I have suffered from pride.

GRANDIER: We must always be on guard.

PHILLIPE: I finished some needlework yesterday, and I was pleased with myself.

GRANDIER: God allows us satisfaction in the work we do.

PHILLIPE: I have been in error through anger.

GRANDIER: Tell me.

PHILLIPE: My sister teased me. I wished her—elsewhere.

GRANDIER: You're absolved. Anything else? (*silence*) Come now, others are waiting.

PHILLIPE: I've had unclean thoughts.

GRANDIER: Of what nature?

PHILLIPE: About a man.

GRANDIER: My child—

PHILLIPE: In the early hours of the morning . . . my bedroom is suffocatingly hot . . . I've asked them to take away the velvet curtains . . . my thoughts fester . . . and yet they are so tender . . . my body . . . Father . . . my body . . . I wish to be touched.

GRANDIER: Have you tried to suppress these thoughts?

PHILLIPE: Yes.

GRANDIER: Are they an indulgence?

PHILLIPE: No. I have prayed.

GRANDIER: Do you wish to be saved from this? (*silence*) Answer, child.

PHILLIPE: No! I want him to take—no, possess—no, destroy me. I love you. Him. I love him!

GRANDIER *comes out from the box: compassion. After a moment he draws aside the curtain and* PHILLIPE *is seen. They stand facing each other.*

DE LA ROCHEPOZAY. ADAM *and* MANNOURY *humbly before him.*

DE LA ROCHEPOZAY: I have considered this document you have presented against the priest, Grandier. He is known to us as an impious and dangerous man. A few months ago we ourselves suffered insult and humiliation by his presence. But this is neither here nor there. What is your complaint?

MANNOURY: We feel, my lord bishop, that Grandier should be forbidden to exercise the sacerdotal function.

DE LA ROCHEPOZAY: What is your profession?

MANNOURY: I'm a surgeon.

DE LA ROCHEPOZAY: Would it amuse you if I came and instructed you in your business?

MANNOURY: I'm always prepared to take advice.

DE LA ROCHEPOZAY: Don't talk like a fool. This grubby and ill-composed document tells us nothing we did not know about the man. Vague and yet somewhat hysterical accusations concerning lonely widows and amorous virgins are all that I can find here. I'm not prepared to conduct the affairs of this diocese on the level of a police court.

ADAM: He has powerful friends.

DE LA ROCHEPOZAY: Stop whispering. What did you say?

ADAM: Grandier is protected by his friends.

DE LA ROCHEPOZAY: What are their names?

MANNOURY (*to Adam: a nudge*): Go on.

ADAM: D'Armagnac. De Cerisay. Others.

DE LA ROCHEPOZAY: I'll accept your reasonable intentions in coming here. Although, God knows, if there's anyone I distrust it's the good citizen going about his civic duty. His motive is usually hate or money. But I will not accept your opinions, your advice, nor, for a moment longer, your presence.

ADAM *and* MANNOURY *go.*

DE LA ROCHEPOZAY (*to his attendant*): It is vital that the Church should be protected from the democratic principle that every man must have his say. Those two probably spoke the truth, but they must not be allowed to think that they influence our judgment in any way.

JEANNE *alone: a book of devotions. Night.* CLAIRE *comes to her.*

CLAIRE: This was just delivered at the gate.

JEANNE *takes a letter from* CLAIRE, *breaks it open, and reads.*

JEANNE: He has refused.

CLAIRE: Father Grandier?

JEANNE (*she reads aloud*): My dear Sister: It is with great regret that I must refuse your invitation to become

Director of your House. The pressing duties I have in the town would not allow me the time to devote my energies to the advantage of your Sisterhood. I very much appreciate all you say of my qualities and . . .

JEANNE *tears the letter across and presses it to her body.*

JEANNE: Thank you, Sister.

CLAIRE *goes.*

JEANNE *alone.*

JEANNE: What is this divine mystery? Let me see. Let me see.

(*laughter*) I was about to address myself to God in this matter. Habit. Habit. It would never do. No. It must be to Man.

She whispers the name: Grandier.

You wake up. Dawn has broken over others before you. Look at the little grey window. Then turn. She lies beside you. The attitude is of prayer or the womb. Her mouth tastes of wine and the sea. Her skin is smooth and silky, rank with sweat. The native odours of her body have exhausted in the night the scents of day.

PHILLIPE, *naked, is seen making love with* GRANDIER. *They will continue to be seen in the touching formal attitudes of passion throughout* JEANNE'S *words.*

ᴊᴀɴɴᴇ: Look down at her. What do you feel? Sadness? It must be sadness. You are a man. Ah, now she stretches her arms above her head. Are you not moved? This is not the sophistry of a whore, whatever you may pretend. She shifts her legs, entwines them, lays a finger on your lips and her mouth upon her finger. She whispers. Those words were taught. She only repeats the lesson. Such filth is love to her, and the speaking of it is an act of faith. (*sudden laughter*) What was that you did? Stretching out to clutch the falling bedclothes. Was it to cover your nakedness? Is there modesty here?

(*silence: in wonder*) How strange. Can you laugh, too? That's something I didn't know. Pain, oblivion, unreason, mania. These I thought would be in your bed. But laughter . . .

How young you both look. Quiet again.

The girl is heavy in your arms. She yawned, and you have taken up the shudder of her body. You tremble, in spite of yourself. Look, the sun is breaking up the mists in the fields. You're going to be engulfed by day. Take what you can. Let both take what they can. Now.

Now.

(*she weeps*) This frenzy, this ripping apart, this meat on a butcher's slab. Where are you? Love? Love? What are you? Now. Now. Now.

ᴊᴇᴀɴᴇ *falls on her knees, convulsed. Grandier and Phillipe can no longer be seen.*

ᴊᴇᴀɴᴇ (*suffocated, young voice*): O my God, is that it? Is that it?

Darkness.

D'ARMAGNAC: DE CERISAY: DE LAUBARDEMONT.

LAUBARDEMONT: It's not a question of compromise. I'm here as His Majesty's Special Commissioner, but I have no power to negotiate. I'm sorry, D'Armagnac.

D'ARMAGNAC: You know, Laubardemont, grown men in this country are getting a little tired of the father figures which keep arising, so we are told, for our own good. France may very well be looked on as a woman, and submissive, but she's not a baby.

LAUBARDEMONT: I'm inclined to agree with you. But I'm not here for argument. I simply brought a message.

D'ARMAGNAC: An order. Pull down the fortifications.

LAUBARDEMONT: That was the message. What answer may I take back?

D'ARMAGNAC: That I refuse.

LAUBARDEMONT: I have a curious feeling.

D'ARMAGNAC: Fear?

LAUBARDEMONT: No, no. Just that you've been influenced in this decision. And that there is pressure behind your obduracy.

D'ARMAGNAC: The decision is entirely mine. As governor of the town.

GRANDIER *approaches.*

D'ARMAGNAC: Do you know Father Grandier?

LAUBARDEMONT: I've heard of him.

D'ARMAGNAC: Well, this is he.

LAUBARDEMONT (*turning*): Ah, Father. Can't you bring your influence to bear on the Governor in this matter of the demolition. As a man of peace I'm sure you want it brought about.

GRANDIER: As a man of peace, I do. As a man of principle, I'd prefer the city walls to remain standing.

LAUBARDEMONT: I see. Well, I seem to be alone in this. If you change your mind, and I earnestly hope you will, I shall be in Loudun for a few days.

LAUBARDEMONT *goes*.

D'ARMAGNAC: Look at him, Grandier.

GRANDIER: A funny little man.

D'ARMAGNAC: My dear fellow, we are all romantic. We see our lives being changed by a winged messenger on a black horse. But more often than not it turns out to be a shabby little man, who stumbles across our path.

A cloister. JEANNE *and* FATHER MIGNON, *a foolish old man, walking together.*

JEANNE: We are all of us so happy, Father Mignon, that you've been able to accept. We shall look forward to having you as our director for many years to come.

MIGNON: You're very kind, my child. You have a direct simplicity which an old man like myself finds very touching.

JEANNE: There are many problems in a place like this. I shall need your advice and guidance.

MIGNON: Always at your disposal.

JEANNE: For example, nearly all the Sisters here are young women. I think you'll agree that youth is more exposed to temptation than age.

MIGNON: That's so. I remember when I was a young man—

JEANNE: I have myself—

MIGNON: What's that?

JEANNE: I was about to say that I have myself recently suffered from visions of a diabolical nature.

MIGNON: In living close to God one becomes a natural prey to the Devil. I shouldn't worry about them too much.

JEANNE: I can speak about this in the daytime. But at night—

MIGNON: It is a well-known fact, my dear, that the spirit is at its weakest in the small hours.

JEANNE: Yes. I managed to resist the vision. Several hours of prayer and I was myself again. But the visitation—

MIGNON: Visitation?

JEANNE: The dead Canon Moussaut, your predecessor, came to me in the night. He stood at the foot of my bed.

MIGNON: But this was a visit of love, my child. Moussaut was a good man. You were fond of him. Did he speak to you?

JEANNE: Yes.

MIGNON: What did he say?

JEANNE: Filth.

MIGNON: What's that?

JEANNE: He spoke filth. Dirt. Jeering, contemptuous, hurtful obscenity.

MIGNON: My beloved Sister—

JEANNE: He was not in his own person.

MIGNON: What do you mean?

JEANNE: He came to me as another. A different man.

MIGNON: Did you recognize this man?

JEANNE: Yes.

MIGNON: Who was it?

JEANNE: Grandier. Father Grandier.

Silence.

MIGNON: My dear, do you understand the seriousness of what you're saying?

JEANNE (*calmly*): Yes. Help me, Father.

GRANDIER: *in the pulpit.*

GRANDIER: . . . For some lewd fellows go about the town and speak against me. I know them. And you will know them when I say that Surgery and Chemistry go hand in hand, vermination against the wall. They have borne false witness. They spy. They sneak. They snigger. And the first sinful man was called Adam, and he begot murder. Why do they pursue me? I am not sick!

If they be here, in this holy place, let them stand before me and declare their hatred, and give the reason for it. I am not afraid to speak openly of what they attempt to discover secretly. If they be in this church let them stand before me. (*silence*) No, they are in some hole in the ground, scratching, so that more venom may come to the surface, and infect us all; distilling bile in retorts; revealing lust, envy and blight with the turn of a scalpel.

During this DE LAUBARDEMONT, *with two attendants, has approached, listened, and moved on.*

O my dear children, I should not speak to you so from this place. And I should not speak to you in bitterness as your pastor.

Do they provoke me to anger? saith the Lord: do they not provoke themselves to the confusion of their own faces?

The pharmacy: ADAM *and* MANNOURY.

ADAM: It's after ten o'clock. Would you believe it?

MANNOURY: Well, we have had a nice talk.

ADAM: Have we got anywhere?

MANNOURY: Somebody at the door.

ADAM: Can't be.

MANNOURY: Is.

ADAM *opens the door.* LAUBARDEMONT *stands there.*

ADAM: No business. Shut.

LAUBARDEMONT: My name is Jean de Martin, Baron de Laubardemont. I am His Majesty's Special Commissioner to Loudun.

ADAM: Can I help you?

LAUBARDEMONT: I hope so.

LAUBARDEMONT *comes into the shop.*

LAUBARDEMONT: I am visiting the town for a kind of investigation.

MANNOURY (*carefully*): We are both honest men.

LAUBARDEMONT: I know. That's why I'm here. I've always found in cases like this that there are perhaps two incorruptible men in the town. Usually close friends, professional men, middle class, backbone of the nation. Deep civic interest. Patriotic. Lost sons in a war. Happily married. Managing to make ends meet in spite of taxation. Austere lives, but what they have they like to be nice. Gentlemen, am I right?

ADAM: Quite correct.

LAUBARDEMONT: Good. I want you to tell me all you know about a man called Grandier. Father Grandier, of Saint Peter's Church.

ADAM: My dear Mannoury, at last!

GRANDIER *and* PHILLIPE: *a secluded place.*

PHILLIPE: I must go home now.

GRANDIER: Yes.

PHILLIPE: I don't like walking through the streets at night. Dogs bark. Listen, they're at it now.

GRANDIER: I wish I could come with you. I would like — oh, words, words!

PHILLIPE: What is it?

GRANDIER: Come here. Gently. I want to tell you—

PHILLIPE: Yes?

GRANDIER: You know the love-making—

PHILLIPE: Yes.

GRANDIER: I want to tell you, Phillipe. Among the clothes dropped on the floor, the soiled linen, the instruction, the apparatus, the surgery—among all this there is a kind of passion of the heart.

PHILLIPE: I know. It is love. Human love.

Silence.

GRANDIER: You understand it that way?

PHILLIPE: I think so.

GRANDIER: Do I love you?

PHILLIPE: I believe so.

GRANDIER: Then what comfort can I give you?

Silence.

PHILLIPE: I am a simple person. I see the world and myself as I have been taught. I am deeply sinful, but my love of God has not deserted me. It is said by Man that those in our state should stand before God. I believe this to be right. And I would not be afraid to declare myself to Him with you beside me, even in our transgression, for I believe Him to be good, wise and always merciful.

Silence.

GRANDIER: You shame me.

The pharmacy. DE LAUBARDEMONT: MANNOURY: ADAM.
They have been joined by FATHER MIGNON.

MIGNON: I couldn't get any more out of the prioress. I can prove nothing. She may be just an hysterical woman.

ADAM: Does it matter?

MIGNON: I'd very much like you, as a surgeon, Mannoury, and you Adam, as a chemist, to be there.

LAUBARDEMONT: May I attend as a disinterested party?

MIGNON: Certainly. If this is a genuine case, the more the— (*he stops*)

LAUBARDEMONT: Were you going to say merrier?

MIGNON: I've sent a message to Father Barré, at Chinon. He's our great local expert in these matters.

MANNOURY: I shall be only too happy to give you any medical advice, Father.

ADAM: And I'll comment on any chemical or biological manifestations.

MIGNON: She already complains of a spasmodic but acute swelling of the belly.

ADAM: Fascinating!

MANNOURY: Not unusual. Sense of false pregnancy. Known it before. Nothing to do with the Devil. Wind?

LAUBARDEMONT: Conjecture is useless. It'll soon be morning.

Dawn. JEANNE *at prayer beside her simple bed.*

JEANNE: Please God, make me a good girl. Take care of my dear father and mother and look after my dog, Captain, who loved me and didn't understand why I had to leave him behind all that time ago. Lord . . . Lord, I would like to make formal prayers to You, but I can only do that out of a book in the chapel. (*silence*) Love me. (*silence*) Love me. Amen.

JEANNE *gets up and goes from the room to a great open space where stand:*

DE LAUBARDEMONT: MANNOURY: ADAM: MIGNON: RANGIER *and* BARRÉ. JEANNE *approaches them.*

BARRÉ: Let me deal with this. Good morning, Sister. Are you well?

JEANNE: I'm very well, thank you, Father.

BARRÉ: Excellent. Will you kneel down?

JEANNE *does so.* BARRÉ *goes to her.*

BARRÉ (*sudden shout*): Are you there! Are you there! (*silence: to the others*) They never answer at once. Afraid of committing themselves. (*to Jeanne*) Come now, declare yourself! In the name of Our Lord Jesus Christ—

Suddenly JEANNE *throws back her crooked head and peals of masculine laughter pour from her open, distorted mouth.*

BARRÉ (*with satisfaction: to the others*): Always does the trick.

JEANNE (*deep man's voice*): Here we are, and here we stay.

BARRÉ: One question.

JEANNE: Pooh!

BARRÉ: Don't be impudent. One question. How did you gain entry to this poor woman?

JEANNE (*deep voice*): Good offices of a friend.

BARRÉ: His name?

JEANNE: Asmodeus.

BARRÉ: That's your name. What is the name of your friend?

JEANNE *is swaying on her knees. She gives inarticulate cries which gradually form themselves into the word:*

JEANNE: Grandier! Grandier! Grandier!

Deep, sullen laughter.

CURTAIN

I I

Saint Peter's Church. Night.

GRANDIER *is at the altar.* PHILLIPE *kneels below him.*

GRANDIER *holds up a salver.* *Speaks:*

GRANDIER: Benedic, ✠ Domine, hunc annulum, quem nos in tuo nomine benedicimus, ✠ ut quae eum gestaverit, fidelitatem integram suo sponso tenens, in pace et voluntate tua permaneat, atque in mutua caritate semper vivat. Per Christum Dominum nostrum.

PHILLIPE: Amen.

GRANDIER *sprinkles the ring with holy water, and then, taking the ring from the salver, comes down to kneel beside Phillipe.*

GRANDIER: With this ring I thee wed: this gold and silver I thee give; with my body I thee worship; and with all my worldly goods I thee endow.

GRANDIER *places the ring on the thumb of Phillipe's hand, saying:*

GRANDIER: In the name of the Father: (*then on the second finger, saying*) And of the Son: (*then on the third finger, saying*) And of the Holy Ghost: (*lastly on the fourth finger, saying*) Amen.

And there he leaves the ring.

GRANDIER *mounts the altar steps.*

GRANDIER: Confirma hoc, Deus, quod operatus es in nobis.

PHILLIPE: A templo sancto tuo, quod est in Jerusalem.

GRANDIER: Kyrie eleison.

PHILLIPE: Christe eleison.

GRANDIER: Kyrie eleison.

They speak together:

Pater noster—
—*and their voices whisper into silence.*

A street.

THE SEWERMAN *is sitting at ease. He holds a cage with a bird in it.*

GRANDIER *and* PHILLIPE *come from the church.*

PHILLIPE: We should step out into the sunlight. Bells should tell the world about us. It shouldn't be night. And as quiet as this. Dear God, my husband, kiss me.

They kiss. THE SEWERMAN *speaks:*

SEWERMAN: So it's done. I saw you go into the church.

GRANDIER: It's done. And well done. Does the bird sing?

SEWERMAN: Not its purpose. Tongueless.

GRANDIER: Do you carry it for love?

SEWERMAN: An idea which would only occur to a good man. Or one careless with hope. No, I carry the thing so that it may die, and I live. He's my saviour. Who's yours?

GRANDIER: You—

SEWERMAN: Blaspheme?

GRANDIER: Yes.

SEWERMAN: Sorry. You know the pits at the edge of the town? Where even your beloved here sends in my buckets. Well, there are days when the place gives off poison. So I always approach it with this creature on a pole before me. His many predecessors have died in the miasma. When this happens I know it's no place for me. So I let the drains run foul for a day or two, and I spend my time catching another victim to shut up here. You'll understand what I mean.

Silence.

GRANDIER: I have put my trust in this child. She is not a victim.

SEWERMAN: Just as you say.

GRANDIER: Come now, even at this hopeless hour you must admit more passes between human beings than the actions which provide you and the laundry with a job.

SEWERMAN: I'm not arguing.

GRANDIER: There is a way of salvation through each other.

SEWERMAN: Are you trying to convince me?

GRANDIER: I'd like to.

SEWERMAN: What about yourself? Has the little ceremony in there done the trick?

GRANDIER: It has given me hope.

SEWERMAN: Hope of what?

GRANDIER: Hope of coming to God by way of a fellow being. Hope that the path, which taken alone, in awful solitude, is a way of despair, can be enlightened by the love of a woman. I have come to believe that by this simple act of committal, which I have done with my heart, it may be possible to reach God by way of happiness.

SEWERMAN: What was that last word?

GRANDIER: Happiness.

SEWERMAN: I don't know what it means. You must have made it up for the occasion. It's getting light.

PHILLIPE: I must go.

SEWERMAN: Yes. They mustn't find the bed empty. On the other hand, they mustn't find it too full.

PHILLIPE (*to Grandier*): Speak to me.

SEWERMAN: Say it.

GRANDIER: I love you, Phillipe.

PHILLIPE *goes.*

SEWERMAN: Speaking of love, some very odd things are going on up at the convent.

GRANDIER: So I'm told.

SEWERMAN: It seems your name is being bandied about by the crazy ladies.

GRANDIER: We must pity them.

SEWERMAN: Will they pity you, that's the point?

GRANDIER: What do you mean? They're deluded.

SEWERMAN: What were you, a few minutes ago, with that girl?

GRANDIER: I was in my right mind, and I knew what I was doing. You may mock me, my son, if you wish.

What seems to you a meaningless act, the marriage of an unmarriageable priest, has meaning for me. The lonely and the proud sometimes need to avail themselves of simple means. I, too, have made fun of the innocent before now. Your debasement has given you an unholy elevation. From your superior position be kind, be wise. Pity me. Pity me.

SEWERMAN: All right. Let's hope the good women of Saint Ursula's will do the same.

Daylight.

JEANNE, *on her knees. Facing her,* BARRÉ, RANGIER *and* MIGNON.

BARRÉ: Exorcise te, immundissime spiritus, omnis incursio adversarii, omne phantasma, omnis legio, in nomine Domini nostri Jesus Christi, eradicare et effugare ab hoc plasmate Dei.

RANGIER *and* MIGNON *come forward.* RANGIER *splashes holy water:* MIGNON *lays on the stole.* ASMODEUS, *in a deep voice, speaks through* JEANNE.

ASMODEUS: You gentlemen are wasting your time. You're soaking the lady, but you're not touching me.

BARRÉ (*to Mignon*): Give me the relic. (MIGNON *hands Barré a small box. It is applied to Jeanne's back*) Adjure te, serpens antique, per judicem vivorum et mortuorum. . . .

ASMODEUS: Excuse me.

BARRÉ: . . . per factorum tuum, per factorum mundi. . . .

ASMODEUS: I'm sorry to interrupt you.

BARRÉ: Well, what is it?

ASMODEUS: I don't understand a word you're saying. I'm a heathen devil. Latin—I suppose it is Latin—is a foreign language to me.

BARRÉ: It is customary to carry out exorcism in Latin.

ASMODEUS: Hidebound, that's what you are. Can't we continue our earlier conversation, which interested me so much, about the sexual activities of priests?

BARRÉ: Certainly not!

ASMODEUS: Is it true that men of your parish . . . (*insane giggles*) . . . is it true that they . . . Bend low. Let me whisper.

JEANNE: O dear God, release this thing from me.

ASMODEUS: Be quiet, woman. You're interrupting a theological discussion.

JEANNE: Father, help me.

BARRÉ: My dear child, I'm doing all I can.

BARRÉ *takes* RANGIER *and* MIGNON *aside: speaks to Rangier.*

BARRÉ: The wretch thinks I'm defeated.

ASMODEUS: You are.

BARRÉ: He seems at the moment to be lodged in the lower bowel. Are Adam and Mannoury here?

RANGIER: They're waiting. In there.

BARRÉ: Ask them to get ready, will you. Consecrate the water, while you're about it.

RANGIER *goes out through the small, low door.* BARRÉ *turns to Jeanne.*

BARRÉ: My beloved Sister, it must be extreme measures.

JEANNE: What do you mean, Father?

BARRÉ: The fiend must be forced from you.

JEANNE: Is there any way, but exorcism?

BARRÉ: Haha! They say the devil takes residence only in the innocent. It's true in this case, it seems. Yes, child, there is another way. (*he shouts*) Do you hear me, Asmodeus?

ASMODEUS (*is it Jeanne's voice?*): Mercy. Mercy.

BARRÉ (*a scream*): Nonsense!

Silence.

RANGIER *comes out from the inner room.*

BARRÉ: My dear boy, you look quite pale. The use of such methods in our job distresses you. Wait till you've been at it as long as I have. Anyway, the Church must keep up with the times. (*to Jeanne*) Come, my dear Sister. Through that little door. There lies your salvation. She looks like a child, doesn't she? Touching. Um. Go along, now. Pretty, pretty. A few steps. (JEANNE *moves forward towards the small door*) Let the power of good propel you. Not much further. There!

JEANNE *is standing in the doorway staring into the small, dark room—and then at once she is struggling in Barré's arms, a howling animal.*

BARRÉ (*powerful: confident*): Help me, Rangier!

RANGIER *comes to Barré, and together they hold the woman.*

JEANNE: No, no! I didn't mean it!

BARRÉ: Too late, Asmodeus. Do you expect mercy now, after your blasphemy and filth against Our Lord?

JEANNE: Father! Father Barré, it is I speaking to you now, Sister Jane of the Angels—

BARRÉ: Ah, Asmodeus, you spoke with many voices.

JEANNE: But it's I, Father. Beloved Mother of this dear convent, protector of little children—

BARRÉ: Silence, beast! Let's get her in there, Rangier. Are you ready, Adam?

ADAM (*from within*): Quite ready.

BARRÉ *and* RANGIER *carry the struggling woman into the room. The door slams shut.* MIGNON, *left alone, gets down on his knees and begins to pray.*

There is a scream from JEANNE *inside the room: it dissolves into sobs and laughter.* MIGNON *prays louder. His empty, excited little voice ascends to nothingness.*

D'ARMAGNAC, DE CERISAY *and* GRANDIER *move into the foreground.*

DE CERISAY: The devil, it seems, departed from the woman at two o'clock precisely.

D'ARMAGNAC: What about the others?

DE CERISAY: The Fathers are working on them now.

D'ARMAGNAC: Same method?

DE CERISAY: No. It seems that after the Prioress more normal methods of exorcism are proving successful. A little holy water—applied externally—a few prayers, and the devils go.

D'ARMAGNAC: Then we can hope for some peace.

DE CERISAY: I don't know.

D'ARMAGNAC: Can't you do something if it starts again? As Magistrate. I'd say such goings-on constitute a civil disorder.

DE CERISAY: I saw Barré and Rangier the other day and questioned the legality of their methods. Next time the convent door was shut in my face. I put myself in a difficult position if I use force against priests. They've asked me to be present at an interrogation of Sister Jane. I'm on my way there now.

D'ARMAGNAC (*to Grandier*): You know your name is constantly being mentioned in this affair.

GRANDIER: Yes, sir.

D'ARMAGNAC: Wouldn't it be a good thing to take steps to clear yourself?

DE CERISAY: Have you offended this woman in some way?

GRANDIER: I don't know how that's possible. I've never seen her.

DE CERISAY: Then why has she chosen you as the devilish perpetrator?

GRANDIER: You look frightened, De Cerisay. Forgive me.

D'ARMAGNAC: You're the one who should be frightened, Father. There was a case some years ago—I forget the man's name—

GRANDIER: I don't, poor devil. There have been many cases, sir.

D'ARMAGNAC: You're in danger.

GRANDIER: Of death? But surely not by a farce such as the convent's putting on. Come, sir, death must be more magnificent, more significant for a man of my kind.

D'ARMAGNAC: How did these other men end?

GRANDIER: At the stake. But they were ridiculous and obscure. Proper matter for sacrifice, that's all.

DE CERISAY: D'Armagnac and I will give you any help we can, Father.

GRANDIER: Can't I talk either of you out of this? When I came here this morning I heard the stories on the streets. I laughed. I thought you'd be doing the same. Is the possession genuine?

DE CERISAY: Not from the evidence I have. As I say, I shall see the woman today. I'll let you know what happens. But you haven't answered my question. Why should it be you?

GRANDIER: Secluded women. They give themselves to God, but something remains which cries out to be given to Man. With the truly pure in heart it can be given in the form of charity, but for the weaker members it is not so easy. It's sad. Very sad, indeed, when you think about it. Imagine being awakened in the night by a quite innocent dream. A dream of your childhood, or of a friend not seen for many years, or even the vision of a good meal. Now, this is a sin. And so you must take up your little whip and scourge your body. We call that discipline. But pain is sensuality, and in its vortex spin images of horror and lust. My beloved Sister in Jesus seems to have fixed her mind on me. There is no reason, De Cerisay. A dropped handkerchief, a scribbled note, a piece of gossip. Any of these things found in the desert of mind and body caused by continual prayer can bring hope. And with hope comes love. And, as we all know, with love comes hate. So I possess this woman. God help her in her terror and unhappiness. God help her. (to D'Armagnac) Now, sir, the business I called on. I've the new plans for your garden summer house. Will you come and see them?   I've revised and modified the frivolity of the design. As you wished.

GRANDIER *and* D'ARMAGNAC *go.* DE CERISAY *stares after them for a moment, and then moves on to enter—*

A high-ceilinged room, furnished with two small beds. One is occupied by JEANNE. BARRÉ, RANGIER *and* MIGNON *are present. Also* ADAM *and* MANNOURY. *A* CLERK *sits writing.*

BARRÉ: Dear Sister in Christ, I must question you further.

JEANNE: Yes, Father.

BARRÉ: Do you remember the first time your thoughts were turned to these evil things?

JEANNE: Very well.

BARRÉ: Tell us.

JEANNE: I was walking in the garden. I stopped. Lying at my feet was a stick of hawthorn. I was sinfully possessed by anger, for that very morning I'd had cause to admonish two of the Sisters for neglecting their duties in the garden. I picked up the unsightly thing in rage. It must have been thorned, for blood ran from my body. Seeing the blood, I was filled with tenderness.

RANGIER: But this revelation may have come from a very different source.

BARRÉ: All the same—(*to the clerk*) Are you getting this down?

JEANNE: There was another time.

BARRÉ: Tell us.

JEANNE: A day or two later. It was a beautiful morning. I'd had a night of dreamless sleep. On the threshold of my room lay a bunch of roses. I picked them up and tucked them into my belt. Suddenly, I was seized by a violent trembling in my right arm. And a great knowledge of love. This persisted throughout my orisons. I was unable to put my mind to anything. It was entirely filled with the representation of a man which had been deeply and inwardly impressed upon me.

BARRÉ: Do you know who sent those flowers?

JEANNE (*long silence: quietly*): Grandier. Grandier.

BARRÉ: What is his rank?

JEANNE: Priest.

BARRÉ: Of what church?

JEANNE: Saint Peter's.

BARRÉ *turns to stare in silence at De Cerisay.*

DE CERISAY (*quietly*): This is nothing.

BARRÉ *turns back to Jeanne.*

BARRÉ: We are unconvinced, my dear Sister. And if our conviction remains untouched I do not have to remind you that you face eternal damnation.

JEANNE *suddenly throws herself across the bed: she utters grunts like a small pig: she grinds her teeth: she disorders the bed. The men draw back from her.* JEANNE *sits upright, staring at them.*

BARRÉ (*with great urgency*): Speak! Speak!

JEANNE: It . . . was . . . night. Day's done!

BARRÉ: Yes?

JEANNE: I had tied back my hair, and scrubbed my face. Back to childhood, eh? Poor Jane. Grown woman. Made for—for. . . .

BARRÉ: Go on.

JEANNE: He came to me.

BARRÉ: Name him!

JEANNE (*at once*): Grandier! Grandier! The beautiful, golden lion entered my room, smiling.

BARRÉ: Was he alone?

JEANNE: No. Six of his creatures were with him.

BARRÉ: Then?

JEANNE: He took me gently in his arms and carried me to the chapel. His creatures each took one of my beloved sisters.

BARRÉ: What took place?

JEANNE (*smiling*): Oh, my dear Father, think of our little chapel, so simple, so unadorned. That night it was a place of luxury and scented heat. Let me tell you. It was full of laughter and music. There were velvets, silks, metals, and the wood wasn't scrubbed, no, not at all. Yes, and there was food. High animal flesh, and wine, heavy, like the fruit from the East. I'd read about it all. How we stuffed ourselves.

DE CERISAY: This is an innocent vision of hell.

BARRÉ: Ssh! Go on.

JEANNE: I forgot. We were beautifully dressed. I wore my clothes as if they were part of my body. Later, when I was naked, I fell among the thorns. Yes, there were thorns strewn on the floor. I fell among them. Come here.

She beckons to BARRÉ, *who leans towards her. She whispers and then laughs.*

BARRÉ (*bleakly*): She says that she and her sisters were compelled to form themselves into an obscene altar, and were worshipped.

JEANNE: Again.

Again she whispers: laughs.

BARRÉ: She says demons tended Grandier, and her beloved sisters incited her. You'll understand what I mean, gentlemen.

JEANNE *again draws Barré to her. She whispers frantically, and gradually her words become audible.*

JEANNE: . . . and so we vanquished God from his house. He fled in horror at the senses fixed in men by another hand. Free of Him, we celebrated His departure again and again. (*she lies back*) To one who has known what I have known, God is dead. I have found peace.

Silence. MIGNON *has fallen on his knees and is praying.* BARRÉ *takes De Cerisay by the arm. As they speak they will move far from Jeanne and the others.*

BARRÉ: This was an innocent woman.

DE CERISAY: That was no devil. She spoke with her own voice. The voice of an unhappy woman, that's all.

BARRÉ: But the degraded imagination and filthy language she used in other depositions. These cannot spring unaided from a cloistered woman. She is a pupil.

DE CERISAY: Of Grandier?

BARRÉ: Yes.

DE CERISAY: But the man swears he's never been in the place.

BARRÉ: Not in his own person.

DE CERISAY: There must be some way of proving what she says. Will you let my people into the house? They will conduct an investigation on a police level.

BARRÉ: Proof? Three of the Sisters have made statements saying that they have undergone copulation with demons and been deflowered. Mannoury has examined them, and it's true that none of them is intact.

DE CERISAY: My dear Father, I don't want to offend your susceptibilities, but we all know about the sentimental attachments which go on between the young women in these places.

BARRÉ: You don't wish to be convinced.

DE CERISAY: I do. Very much. One way or another.

DE CERISAY *goes*. BARRÉ *turns*. MANNOURY *and* ADAM *are approaching*.

ADAM: Well, there, now.

MANNOURY: Fascinating.

ADAM: Unusual.

MANNOURY: Must say. Hell can't be as dull as some people make out. Haha! What?

ADAM: Such things.

MANNOURY: You know, I think a privately printed testament of this case might have quite a sale. Shall we write it up?

ADAM: Let's.

They have approached Barré.

BARRÉ: Have you examined her?

MANNOURY: Yes. I'll let you have my report later.

BARRÉ: Can you give me anything to go on, meantime?

MANNOURY: As a professional man—

ADAM: He speaks for me.

MANNOURY: I don't like to commit myself.

BARRÉ: Even so—

MANNOURY: Well, let's put it this way. There's been hanky-panky.

BARRÉ: Don't mince words. There's been fornication!

MANNOURY: Rather!

BARRÉ: Lust! She's been had!

ADAM: I'll say.

BARRÉ: Thank you, gentlemen. That's all I need. Look.

They are silent. GRANDIER *is walking in the distance.* BARRÉ, MANNOURY *and* ADAM *go.*

GRANDIER *approaches.* PHILLIPE *comes quickly to him.*

PHILLIPE: They said you were at the Governor's house.

GRANDIER: I've just come from there. What's the matter?

PHILLIPE: I want to know. Was I restless last night? I had to leave you before it was light. I went as quietly as as I could. Did I disturb you? It's important that I should know.

GRANDIER: I can't remember. Why is it important?

PHILLIPE: You can't remember.

She gives a sudden, startling, harsh laugh.

GRANDIER: Walk to the church with me.

PHILLIPE: No.

GRANDIER: Very well.

PHILLIPE: There's no need to go into the confessional to say what I have to tell you. I'm pregnant.

Silence.

GRANDIER: So it ends.

PHILLIPE: I'm frightened.

GRANDIER: Of course. How can I own the child?

PHILLIPE: I'm very frightened.

GRANDIER: And there was such bravery in love, wasn't there, Phillipe? All through the summer nights. How unafraid we were each time we huddled down together. We laughed as we roused the animal. Remember? Now it has devoured us.

PHILLIPE: Help me.

GRANDIER: And we were to have been each other's salvation. Did I really believe it was possible?

PHILLIPE: I love you.

GRANDIER: Yes, I did believe it. I remember leaving you one day—you had been unusually adroit—

PHILLIPE: O God!

GRANDIER: I was filled with that indecent confidence which comes after perfect coupling. And as I went I thought—yes, solemnly I thought—the body can transcend its purpose. It can become a thing of such purity that it can be worshipped to the limits of imagination. Anything is allowed. All is right. And such perfection makes for an understanding of the hideous state of existence.

PHILLIPE: Touch me.

GRANDIER: But what is it now? An egg. A thing of weariness, loathing and sickness. So it ends.

PHILLIPE: Where is love?

GRANDIER: Where, indeed? Go to your father. Tell him the truth. Let him find some good man. They exist.

PHILLIPE: Help me.

GRANDIER: How can I help you? Take my hand. There. Like touching the dead, isn't it? Goodbye, Phillipe.

GRANDIER *goes*.

The pharmacy. ADAM, MANNOURY *and* FATHER MIGNON.

There is a harsh cry from FATHER BARRÉ *as he appears at the top of the stairway. He moves like a drunken man. The others scatter in alarm.*

BARRÉ: I was denied entrance to the convent tonight. By armed guards.

MIGNON: My God, my God, what's wrong?

BARRÉ: The Archbishop has issued an ordinance against further exorcism or investigation.

MIGNON: Never!

BARRÉ: It was done at the request of De Cerisay and D'Armagnac. What's more, the Archbishop's personal physician—that rationalist fool!—got hold of the women without my knowledge. He examined them, and gave it as his opinion that there was no genuine possession.

MIGNON: What shall we do? Oh, what shall we do?

BARRÉ *comes down into the room.*

BARRÉ: De Cerisay sees it as an act of justice. He doesn't understand that such things play straight into the hands of the devil. Allow reasonable doubt for a man's sin, and the devil snaps it up. (*he shouts wearily*) There can be no reasonable doubt in sin. All or nothing!

MIGNON: Of course. Of course. Justice has nothing to do with salvation. Sit down. Sit down.

BARRÉ: My life's work is threatened by a corrupt archbishop, a liberal doctor and an ignorant lawyer. Ah, gentlemen, there'll be happiness in hell tonight.

Silence.

MANNOURY: Are we done for, then?

ADAM: Seems so.

MANNOURY: All up.

ADAM: Dear me.

MANNOURY: Pity.

MIGNON: Let us pray.

ADAM: I beg your pardon?

MIGNON: Let us pray.

ADAM: What for?

MIGNON: Well, let me think—

ADAM: Right you are.

MIGNON: I know!

ADAM: Yes?

MIGNON: Let us pray that the Archbishop has a diabolic vision. . . .

BARRÉ (*to Mannoury*): I shall go back to my parish.

MIGNON (*to Adam*): . . . of a particularly horrible nature. . . .

BARRÉ (*to Mannoury*): There's work for me there.

MIGNON (*to Adam*): He's an old man, too. Perhaps we can frighten him to death.

BARRÉ: Be quiet, Mignon. You rave.

MIGNON: Don't leave us.

BARRÉ: I must.

MIGNON: You're naturally a little depressed by this set-back. But we'll find a way.

BARRÉ: No. The Archbishop's ordinance has made evil impossible in this place. For the moment. But the ordinance doesn't apply in my parish, and you can be sure that Satan is trumpeting there. I must answer the call.

MIGNON: We shall miss you very much.

BARRÉ: My dear friend, a whisper from hell and I shall be back.

D'ARMAGNAC *and* DE CERISAY *at a table.* GRANDIER *formally approaches them.*

GRANDIER: I believe I must thank you, De Cerisay, for having this persecution stopped. Very well. I do so now.

DE CERISAY: I acted for you, Father, but not entirely on your behalf. The circus up at the convent was beginning to attract a lot of unwelcome attention to the town. It's my job to keep some sort of order in the place.

D'ARMAGNAC: You don't make it easy for your friends, Grandier. Trincant has told me about his daughter. You have your whores. Why did you have to do this?

GRANDIER: It seemed a way.

D'ARMAGNAC: A way to what?

GRANDIER: All worldly things have a single purpose for a man of my kind. Politics, power, the senses, riches, pride and authority. I choose them with the same care that you, sir, select a weapon. But my intention is different. I need to turn them against myself.

D'ARMAGNAC: To bring about your end?

GRANDIER: Yes. I have a great need to be united with God. Living has drained the need for life from me. My exercise of the senses has flagged to total exhaustion. I am a dead man, compelled to live.

D'ARMAGNAC: You disgust me. This is a sickness.

GRANDIER: No, sir. It is the meaning and purpose.

D'ARMAGNAC: I'm not one for sophisticated argument, but tell me something. I can see that the obvious short cut, self-destruction, is not possible. But isn't creating the circumstances for your death, which is what you seem to be doing, equally sinful?

GRANDIER: Leave me some hope.

D'ARMAGNAC: The hope that God will smile upon your efforts to create an enemy so malignant as to bring you down, and so send you—up?

GRANDIER: Yes.

D'ARMAGNAC: I've a letter here from Paris. It should
make you happy. By supporting me in this matter of
the fortifications you have made an excellent enemy.
Richelieu. So far the King is standing with me against
the Cardinal. But should the King fail or falter this
city will come down, and you will probably have your
wish, for you are deeply implicated. All the same, I
shall continue to protect you from what I think to be a
most dreadful course, and a most blasphemous philoso-
phy.

GRANDIER: It is what I seek, sir. Don't hold it from me.
Think what it must be like. I reach the end of a long
day. I am warm, fed and satisfied. I go home. On the
way I stare at a stranger across the street, perhaps a
child. I greet a friend. I lie looking down on the face
of a sleeping woman. I see these with wonder and hope,
and ask myself: Is this, perhaps, the means to my end?
And I am denied.

GRANDIER *suddenly hides his face in his hands.*

GRANDIER: O my God, my God! All things fail me.

D'ARMAGNAC: Afraid, Grandier?

GRANDIER: Yes. Yes. Yes. Forsaken.

The convent garden. JEANNE *and* CLAIRE *are sitting on a
bench.* LOUISE *and* GABRIELLE *are on the ground at their
feet. Two lay sisters stand nearby. Great stillness.*

LOUISE: What shall we do, Mother?

JEANNE: Do?

LOUISE: People are taking their children away from us.

JEANNE: Who can blame them?

CLAIRE: There's no one to help. We have to do all the housework ourselves. It's very tiring.

JEANNE (*sudden laughter*): Why don't you ask the devils to lend a hand?

CLAIRE: Mother!

GABRIELLE: I've taken in a little washing and sewing. I hope you don't mind, Mother.

JEANNE: Sensible girl. When hell fails to provide one can fall back on hard work, eh?

GABRIELLE: I know you've never liked us to do menial tasks.

JEANNE: I said it diminished women in our vocation. (*she laughs*) Did I say that?

GABRIELLE: Yes.

Silence.

LOUISE: Mother—

JEANNE: Yes, child?

LOUISE: Why has the Archbishop forbidden Father Barré to come and see us any more?

JEANNE: Because the Archbishop has been told that we are foolish and deluded women.

LOUISE: Mother—

JEANNE: Yes?

LOUISE: Have we sinned?

JEANNE: By what we've done?

ᴊᴇ: Yes. Have we mocked God?

ᴀɴɴᴇ: It was not the intention.

But to make a mockery of Man. That's a different matter!

For what a splendid creature he makes to be fooled. He might have been created for no other purpose. With his head in the air, besotted with his own achievement, he asks to be tripped. Deep in the invention of mumbo-jumbo to justify his existence, he is deaf to laughter. With no eyes for anything but himself, he's blind to the gesture of ridicule made in front of his face.

So, drunk, deaf and blind, he goes on. The perfect subject for the practical joke. And that, my sisters, is where the children of misfortune — like me — play a part. We do not mock our beloved Father in Heaven. Our laughter is kept for His wretched and sinful children who get above their station, and come to believe they have some other purpose in this world than to die.

After the delusions of power come the delusions of love. When men cannot destroy they start to believe they can be saved by creeping into a fellow human being. And so perpetuating themselves. Love me, they say over and over again, love me. Cherish me. Defend me. Save me. They say it to their wives, their whores, their children, and some to the whole human race. Never to God. These are probably the most ridiculous of all, and most worthy of derision. For they do not understand the glory of mortality, the purpose of man: loneliness and death.

Let us go in.

On the fortifications. Night.

D'ARMAGNAC *and* DE CERISAY *enter from different ways. They are wrapped against the rain, and they shout above the wind.*

DE CERISAY: D'Armagnac, are you there?

D'ARMAGNAC: The horseman fell at the gate. They found these papers, scattered.

DE CERISAY: What are they?

D'ARMAGNAC: The king has gone back on his word. Richelieu has won. The town fortifications are to come down. It is to be a little place. I shall have no more power than a tradesman.

GRANDIER *has appeared far below them.*

D'ARMAGNAC: Is that the priest?

DE CERISAY: Yes. (*he shouts*) Grandier!

D'ARMAGNAC: He will suffer. (*he shouts*) Grandier!

GRANDIER: What's the matter?

D'ARMAGNAC: The Cardinal has moved against us.

DE CERISAY: The King has lost his nerve.

D'ARMAGNAC: All this is to come down.

DE CERISAY: You are mentioned—

D'ARMAGNAC: We shan't stand here much longer.

DE CERISAY: —named for your resistance.

D'ARMAGNAC: You are in danger.

GRANDIER: Thank God.

D'ARMAGNAC: What do you say? I can't hear you. Are you mad? Is he mad? Let's go down.

D'ARMAGNAC *and* DE CERISAY *go.* GRANDIER *kneels. The wind and rain sweep about him.*

GRANDIER: Heavenly Father, You have restored strength to my enemies, and hope to Your sinful child. I give myself into the hands of the world secure in the faith of Your mysterious ways. You have made the way possible. I understand, and I accept. But You work beyond a curtain of majesty. I am afraid to raise my eyes, and see. Reveal Yourself. Reveal Yourself.

His voice is lost.

Stillness.

DE LAUBARDEMONT *and* MIGNON.

LAUBARDEMONT: We shall have to act quickly.

MIGNON: Yes. Yes.

LAUBARDEMONT: I must start for Paris tonight.

MIGNON: So soon?

LAUBARDEMONT: Can it be done in the time?

MIGNON: We must try.

LAUBARDEMONT: Sort out your thoughts on the subject.

MIGNON: I've been reading it up. There was the appalling Gauffridy case. In Marseilles, twenty years ago. The priest bewitched and debauched several Ursulines—

LAUBARDEMONT: We don't need precedents. We need results. Here and now. Call them in.

MIGNON *leads* JEANNE *forward. They are followed by* CLAIRE, LOUISE, GABRIELLE *and the two lay sisters.* DE LAUBARDEMONT *stands apart.*

MIGNON: My beloved sisters in Christ, I am only a foolish old man who hasn't much time left on this earth to do God's will—

LAUBARDEMONT: Well then, get on with it.

MIGNON: My children, do you trust me?

JEANNE: Of course, Father.

MIGNON: As your spiritual instructor, do you trust me?

JEANNE: Always.

MIGNON: Very well. I am deeply disturbed by this sudden cessation of diabolical manifestations in you. Dreadful stories are being put about in the town and farther afield. They say you were not truly possessed by demons, but that you were playing parts, making a mockery both of your sublime state, and your superiors in the Church.

JEANNE: That is what we were told by the Archbishop's doctor. He talked about hysteria. The cry from the womb.

MIGNON: But as a good woman it was up to you to prove him wrong. Oh, assure me that it was true. You were possessed.

JEANNE: It was true. We were possessed by hell.

MIGNON: And the instigator, the foul magician—

JEANNE: Grandier! Grandier!

THE SISTERS: Grandier! Grandier!

MIGNON: But now I fear for you in another way. The evidence is all against you. The silence of the devils condemns you.

Silence.

MIGNON: You see, they do not speak. There is no proof of your virtue. Ah, my sisters, this stillness presages your eternal damnation. I fear for you. I dread. Forsaken by God and forsaken by the Devil you stand in the most desolate limbo for ever. I beg you, consider your position.

JEANNE: Father, we are afraid.

MIGNON: And well you may be, my child.

JEANNE: Don't leave us!

MIGNON: What else can I do? I will pray for you.

MIGNON *turns away towards De Laubardemont.*

LEVIATHAN (*speaking through Jeanne*): May I put in a word?

MIGNON: God be praised! What is your name?

LEVIATHAN: Leviathan.

MIGNON: Where are you lodged, unholy thing?

LEVIATHAN: In the lady's forehead.

BEHERIT (*speaking through Jeanne*): I am in the woman's stomach. My name is Beherit.

ISACAARON (*speaking through Jeanne*): Isacaaron speaking. From under the last rib on the left.

ELYMI (*speaking through Claire*): I am here. (*another voice*)
And I.

EAZAZ (*speaking through Louise*): And I. (*another voice*) And
I am here.

*Clamour of diabolical voices.   Derisive laughter: grunts, squeals,
howls.*

DE LAUBARDEMONT *moves to Mignon.*

LAUBARDEMONT: Well done.   Barré must be got back
from Chinon.   He must begin exorcism at once.   In
public.   A representative of the Court will attend.   See
to it.

DE LAUBARDEMONT *goes.*   MIGNON *runs forward, shouting:*

MIGNON: Open the gates!   Open the gates!

*A crowd floods into the palace.   Men and women of the town.
The Sewerman.   Adam and Mannoury.   Trincant.   A dwarf.
A creature.   A trumpeter.   Laughing women.   Dogs.   Children
climb to points of vantage and look down.*

Below: the Sisters laboriously perform their antics. JEANNE *is on
her hands and knees, snuffling the ground.* CLAIRE *has the
skirts of her habit over her head, exposing herself in a dull
promenade.* LOUISE *and* GABRIELLE *are locked in an em-
brace, making a beast.   And from all of them come the hoarse,
masculine cries of diabolic voices: inarticulate, whining, com-
manding, a dissonance of obscenity.*

*The townspeople are very amused.   They point out especially
delectable gestures to each other.   Some urge the Sisters to greater
excesses.   A lay sister, agile as a tumbler, is applauded.   A
party has settled down to eat and drink and watch.*

Thunder of bells from Saint Peter's spire.

BARRÉ *enters in glory. He carries a gold, jewelled crucifix, which twists and glitters in his nervous hands.* RANGIER *comes from another way.* THREE CARMELITES *from another.* MIGNON *approaches them. All meet.*

BARRÉ: I have been sent for.

MIGNON: Yes. Yes.

BARRÉ: The triumph of good!

MIGNON: It is. Yes.

BARRÉ: De Cerisay—

MIGNON: Bah!

BARRÉ: D'Armagnac—

MIGNON: Filth!

BARRÉ: Are they here?

MIGNON: No.

RANGIER: Dare not show their faces.

BARRÉ: The triumph of good! I am in love with the words. I must say them again. It is the triumph of good!

A LAY SISTER *is scrabbling at Barré's feet.*

BARRÉ: Peace, Sister.

BARRÉ *lays on the crucifix. It has no effect, so he savagely kicks the woman aside.*

RANGIER: The King's man is here.

BARRÉ: Who have they sent?

RANGIER: Prince Henri de Condé.

BARRÉ: One of the blood!

RANGIER: No less.

BARRÉ: Excellent. (*he shouts*) Constables!

ARCHERS *enter, and press back the crowd. Near silence. The archers range themselves against the crowd, isolating the Sisters.*

LEVIATHAN (*speaking through Jeanne in a loud voice*): Where is the enemy?

BARRÉ (*in great exaltation*): I am here.

LEVIATHAN: Who are you?

BARRÉ: I am only a humble man. But I speak for the Lord Jesus Christ.

A terrible scream from LEVIATHAN. *Babel of voices from the other devils. Delight of the crowd.*

BARRÉ: Mignon: water, a missal, the stoles, the ciborium, the saint's fingernail, the piece of the true cross. Let me have them all.

MIGNON: God's armoury! It's here.

THE CARMELITES *have brought forward and are arranging the relics.*

BARRÉ: I must prepare myself.

BARRÉ *falls on his knees: prays. The crowd is silent.*

HENRI DE CONDÉ *enters. This exquisite and handsome sodomite is supported by painted boys. He regards Barré for a moment: speaks.*

DE CONDÉ: I don't wish, my dear Father, to disturb your devotions, and I would never suggest that a member of the royal family took precedence over God . . . all the same. . . .

BARRÉ (*he has got to his feet*) : I'm at your service, sir.

DE CONDÉ: Thank you. These are the raving women, I take it.

BARRÉ: All of them are possessed by one or more devils.

DE CONDÉ: And the instigator is a man of your own people?

BARRÉ: A priest, yes.

DE CONDÉ: You don't seem amused.

BARRÉ: Amused?

DE CONDÉ: Never mind.

BARRÉ: If you'll take your place, sir, I'll proceed.

DE CONDÉ: Very well.

DE CONDÉ *goes to a prepared part nearby, and sits overlooking the scene. The boys play around him like butterflies.*

The Sisters are now in an untidy heap, exhausted, mere rubbish on the ground. BARRÉ *is robing and preparing himself with the help of* MIGNON *and* RANGIER.

DE CONDÉ *draws one of the boys to him.*

DE CONDÉ These are women, darling. Look well. Vomit, if you wish. Man is born of them. Gross things. Nasty. Breeding ground. Eggs hatch out in hot dung. Don't wrinkle your little nose, pet. Take this scent. Some men love them. The priest, Grandier, for example. He's picked the gobbets from the stew. He's—(DE CONDÉ *whispers in the boy's ear. The child's eyes widen.* DE CONDÉ *laughs.*)

BARRÉ *has come forward.*

BARRÉ: With your permission, sir, I'll begin.

DE CONDÉ: Please do so.

BARRÉ: But first I have a declaration to make. This, sir— (*he holds up the ciborium*)—contains the holy eucharist.

BARRÉ *places the ciborium on his head and kneels.*

BARRÉ: Heavenly Father, I pray that I may be confounded and that the maledictions of Dathan and Abiram may fall upon me, if I have sinned or been at fault in any way in this affair.

DE CONDÉ: A very commendable gesture. Bravo!

BARRÉ *rises, and goes towards Jeanne.*

BARRÉ: Leviathan! Leviathan!

LEVIATHAN (*speaking through Jeanne: sleepy*): Go away.

BARRÉ: Rouse yourself.

LEVIATHAN (*speaking through Jeanne*): You bore me.

BARRÉ: In the name of Our Lord Jesus Christ—

LEVIATHAN (*speaking through Jeanne*): Don't keep bringing that impostor's name into the conversation.

BARRÉ: It disturbs you, eh?

LEVIATHAN (*speaking through Jeanne*): I don't tolerate fools gladly. All that talk about love. It has a softening effect on the character. And what's more, the fellow wasn't a gentleman.

DE CONDÉ: Reverend Father—

BARRÉ: Yes, sir?

DE CONDÉ: I notice that you don't speak to these creatures in Latin, as is usual. Why is that?

BARRÉ: They're not conversant with the language. You'll understand, sir, that there are uneducated as well as educated devils.

DE CONDÉ: Quite.

LEVIATHAN (*speaking through Jeanne*): I haven't travelled much.

Deep laughter, taken up by the other devils.

BARRÉ: Listen, Filth—

LEVIATHAN (*speaking through Jeanne*): You're always so personal.

BARRÉ: I'm going to speak a name to you. Grandier!

LEVIATHAN (*speaking through Jeanne*): Oh, that's a sweet noise. Do it again.

BARRÉ: Grandier!

LEVIATHAN (*speaking through Jeanne*): Yes, I like that.

BARRÉ: You know him?

LEVIATHAN (*speaking through Jeanne*): We serve him. Don't we?

ZABULON (*speaking through Claire*): Yes.

ISACAARON (*speaking through Jeanne*): We do. We do.

BEHERIT (*speaking through Jeanne*): Grandier! Grandier!

EAZAZ (*speaking through Louise*): Oh, my love, my darling, hold me, take—take—aah!—

ZABULON (*speaking through Claire*): Grandier! Grandier!

BEHERIT (*speaking through Jeanne*): Grandier! Grandier!

EAZAZ (*speaking through Louise*): Grandier! Grandier!

LEVIATHAN (*speaking through Jeanne*): Grandier! Grandier!

Pandemonium.

BARRÉ: Let one speak for all!

RANGIER *and* MIGNON *move in among the Sisters scattering holy water. The screams and shouts gradually die away.*

DE CONDÉ: Father, may I question these things?

BARRÉ: By all means, sir,

RANGIER, MIGNON *and the* CARMELITES *hustle the wretched Sisters forward until they are ranged in front of* DE CONDÉ, *who stares down at them.*

DE CONDÉ (*addressing the Sisters*): Gentlemen. You have given us your views on the character and worth of our blessed Saviour. (*hissing from the devils*) Which of you will answer me on a matter of merely national importance?

BEHERIT (*speaking through Jeanne*): I'll try.

DE CONDÉ: You will? Good. What's your name?

BEHERIT (*speaking through Jeanne*): Beherit.

DE CONDÉ Well, Beherit, tell me this. What's your opinion of His Majesty, the King of France, and his adviser, the great Cardinal?

Silence.

DE CONDÉ: Come now, as a political devil you must have some views. Or do you find yourself in the quandary of most Oppositions? Having to speak with more than one voice.

BEHERIT (*speaking through Jeanne: muttering*): Don't understand.

DE CONDÉ: You understand very well. If you, Beherit, praise the King and his minister you condone, and imply that their policy is hellish. If you, Sister Jane, dispraise them, you run the risk of treason against powerful men. I sympathise with your difficulty. Father Barré—

BARRÉ *comes forward, as* DE CONDÉ *takes a small box from one of the boys.*

DE CONDÉ: I have here a relic of the most holy worth. It has been lent to me by a great cathedral of the north. I feel the bits and pieces which you've assembled from local sources may not be powerful enough to dispel these impudent demons. So why not try this?

BARRÉ: What is in the box, sir?

DE CONDÉ: A phial of the blood of our Lord Jesus Christ.

BARRÉ *reverently takes the box in his hands: kisses it.*

DE CONDÉ: Tell me, Father, what effect would the close proximity of this relic have on devils such as these?

BARRÉ: It would put them to flight.

DE CONDÉ: At once?

BARRÉ: Immediately. I couldn't guarantee, of course, that when the relic was removed they wouldn't return.

DE CONDÉ: Of course not. That would be asking too much. Would you like to try?

BARRÉ *goes towards Jeanne.*

BARRÉ: In the name of our Heavenly Father, I conjure thee, most frightful beings, by this most sacred substance, to depart!

BARRÉ *applies the box to Jeanne's forehead. At once, in a number of horrible screams, the devils leave her body by way of her distorted mouth. Silence. Then* JEANNE *rises to her full height. She speaks calmly, with the voice of a young girl, in her own person.*

JEANNE: I am free. I am free.

She goes to DE CONDÉ, *kneels, and kisses his hands.*

DE CONDÉ: I'm very pleased to have been of some service, madam.

BARRÉ (*triumphantly*): You see!

DE CONDÉ *takes the box from* BARRÉ, *opens it, and holds it upside down: it is empty.*

DE CONDÉ: You see, Father?

BARRÉ (*after a moment*): Ah, sir, what sort of trick have you played on us?

DE CONDÉ: Reverend Sir, what sort of trick are you playing on *us*?

Silence between the two men, DE CONDÉ *smiling: hushed crowd: terrified women.*

The moment is broken by MIGNON. *He starts to run in tiny circles, holding his little head in his hands.*

LEVIATHAN (*speaking through Mignon*): Fooled again!

BEHERIT (*speaking through Mignon*): Make way!

MIGNON *cries out, as Beherit forces an entry.*

RANGIER *suddenly begins to neigh like a horse, and high stepping in fine style, proceeds to exhibit.* THE SISTERS *begin to grunt and groan in sympathy, one of them offering herself obscenely to* RANGIER, *who mounts. Only* JEANNE *stands alone and still.* A BOY *by De Condé begins to laugh in a ringing, hysterical way. There is a disturbance in the crowd. Two women have become possessed.*

BARRÉ *stares about him in horror. Then, wielding the crucifix like a club, he plunges among the devils, laying about him.*

BARRÉ: We are besieged! Clear the place at once!

The CARMELITES *hurry away the Sisters, and the dancing Mignon and Rangier. The guards disperse the crowd.* BARRÉ *is passing among the people, laying the cross on possessed and unpossessed alike, and shouting:*

BARRÉ: . . . per factorem mundi, per eum qui habet potestatem mittendi te in gehennam, ut ab hoc famulo Dei, qui ad sinum Ecclesiae recurrit, cum metu et exercitu furoris tui festinus discedas.

RANGIER, MIGNON *and* THE SISTERS *go into the distance, followed by* BARRÉ. *The crowd go yawning home.*

THE BOY *standing beside* DE CONDÉ *still laughs himself to tears.*

DE CONDÉ (*smiling*): Be quiet, child.

DE CONDÉ *stares across at* JEANNE, *who stands alone, some way off.*

DE CONDÉ: Mother, I am often accused of libertinage. Very well. Being born so high I have to stoop lower than other men. Soiled, dabbling myself, I know what I am doing and what I must give. I'd say you'll have your wish about this man Grandier, seeing the way the world goes. But do you know what you must give? (*casually*) Your immortal soul to damnation in an infinite desert of eternal bestiality.

DE CONDÉ *and* THE BOYS *go.*

CLAIRE *and* LOUISE *enter apart from* JEANNE. *Gay voices.*

CLAIRE: I was never any good at prayer.

LOUISE: Neither was I.

CLAIRE: We could have spent our lives on our knees.

LOUISE: And no one would have heard of us.

CLAIRE: They're selling my picture in the town.

LOUISE· We're famous all over France.

CLAIRE: Are you still worried about being damned?

LOUISE: Not any more.

CLAIRE: Not since your beautiful legs have been so admired .

LOUISE: Sweetheart, what do you think of in chapel now?

CLAIRE: This and that. New ways.

LOUISE: To amuse?

CLAIRE: Yes. (*a bell*) Come on.

Laughing, they go. JEANNE *stands silent for a moment. Then:*

LEVIATHAN (*speaking through Jeanne*): Clear your mind of cant, you absurd little monster.

JEANNE: I'm afraid.

LEVIATHAN (*speaking through Jeanne*): Nonsense. We'll support you in anything you do.

JEANNE: I wish to be pure.

LEVIATHAN (*speaking through Jeanne*): There is no such thing.

JEANNE: O God: God, yes, there is.

Women's voices are raised from the nearby chapel.

LEVIATHAN (*speaking through Jeanne*): No, there isn't. Now
think, my dear. Remember the night time visions. He
and—(*obscene giggles*)—oh, that thing—and you,
agape—no, no, my darling, not purity, not even dignity.
What are you thinking of? Not only all impure, but all
absurd. Remember?

JEANNE *starts to laugh:* LEVIATHAN *joins her.*

Darkness.

A Council of State. Night.

LOUIS XIII, RICHELIEU, FATHER JOSEPH *and* LA
VRILLIERE, *Secretary of State.*

DE CONDÉ *is apart.*

DE LAUBARDEMONT *comes forward and speaks to the Council.
A clerk stands beside him, handing over relevant papers from
time to time.*

LAUBARDEMONT: Your Majesty. Your Eminence. You
have asked me to report on the case of possession at
Loudun. The man's name is Urbain Grandier.

DE CONDÉ: He is innocent.

Both men speak to the Council.

LAUBARDEMONT: I have been advised by priests of the
district and by reputable medical men that the possession
is genuine.

DE CONDÉ: I have also been there. The man is innocent.

LAUBARDEMONT: Grandier's house has been searched. Various manuscripts have been found. There was a pamphlet written some years ago and directed against Your Eminence. Other papers confirmed Grandier's support of D'Armagnac in his defiant attitude about the fortifications of the town, which has distressed you so much, Your Majesty. There were letters and notebooks of a more personal kind. A treatise on Sacerdotal Celibacy was found. The man seems to have been in love when this was written. It is reported that a mock marriage took place with a daughter of the Public Prosecutor. There were letters from other women, one of which appears to suggest that he has committed the veneric act in church.

DE CONDÉ: For the love of Jesus Christ, if you wish to destroy the man, then destroy him. I'm not here to plead for his life. But your methods are shameful. He deserves better. Any man does. Kill him with power, but don't pilfer his house, and hold evidence of this sort against him. What man could face arraignment on the idiocy of youth, old love letters, and the pathetic objects stuffed in drawers or at the bottom of cupboards, kept for the fear that one day he would need to be reminded that he was once loved? No. Destroy a man for his opposition, his strength or his majesty. But not for this!

Silence.

LAUBARDEMONT (*to the Council*): I should now give you any evidence in the man's favour. . . . (*he is interrupted by a sign from Richelieu*)

RICHELIEU: The Devil must never be believed, even when he tells the truth.

LAUBARDEMONT: I shall act on your instructions at once.

DE LAUBARDEMONT *comes forward.* GUARDS *gather about him. They move off.*

A brilliant morning.

GRANDIER *comes to the Sewerman, carrying flowers.*

SEWERMAN: Why, whatever's this?

GRANDIER: I must have picked them somewhere. I can't remember. You have them.

SEWERMAN: Thank you. They smell sweet. Very suitable.

GRANDIER: Can I sit with you?

SEWERMAN: Of course. I've no sins this morning, though. Sorry.

GRANDIER: Let me look at you.

SEWERMAN: Do you like what you see?

GRANDIER: Very much.

SEWERMAN: What's happened? You're drunk with mystery.

GRANDIER: I've been out of the town. An old man was dying. I sat with him for two nights and a day. I was seeing death for the hundredth time. It was an obscene struggle. It always is. Once again a senile, foolish and sinful old man had left it rather late to come to terms. He held my hand so tightly that I could not move. His grimy face stared up at me in blank surprise at what was happening to him. So I sat there in the rancid smell of the kitchen, while in the darkness the family argued in whispers, between weeping, about how much money there would be under the bed.

He was dirty and old and not very bright. And I loved him so much. I envied him so much, for he was standing on the threshold of everlasting life. I wanted him to turn his face to God, and not peer back through the smoky light, and stare longingly at this mere preliminary. I said to him: Be glad, be glad. But he did not understand.

His spirit weakened at dawn. It could not mount another day. There were cries of alarm from the family. I took out the necessary properties which I travel in this bag. The vulgar little sins were confessed, absolved, and the man could die. He did so. Brutally, holding on to the last. I spoke my usual words to the family, with my priest's face. My duty was done.

But I could not forget my love for the man.

I came out of the house. I thought I'd walk back, air myself after the death cell. I was very tired. I could hear Saint Peter's bell.

The road was dusty. I remembered the day I came here. I was wearing new shoes. They were white with dust. Do you know, I flicked them over with my stole before being received by the bishop. I was vain and foolish, then. Ambitious, too.

I walked on. They were working in the fields and called to me. I remembered how I loved to work with my hands when I was a boy. But my father said it was unsuitable for one of my birth.

I could see my church in the distance. I was very proud, in a humble way. I thought of my love for the beauty of this not very beautiful place. And I remembered night in the building, with the gold, lit by candlelight, against the darkness.

I thought of you. I remembered you as a friend.

I rested. The country was stretched out. Do you know where the rivers join? I once made love there.

Children came past me. Yes, of course, that's where I got the flowers. I didn't pick them. They were given to me.

I watched the children go. Yes, I was very tired. I could see far beyond the point my eyes could see. Castles, cities, mountains, oceans, plains, forests—and—

And then—oh, my son, my son—and then—I want to tell you—

SEWERMAN: Do so. Be calm.

GRANDIER: My son, I—Am I mad?

SEWERMAN: No. Quite sane. Tell me. What did you do?

GRANDIER: I created God!

Silence.

GRANDIER: I created Him from the light and the air, from the dust of the road, from the sweat of my hands, from gold, from filth, from the memory of women's faces, from great rivers, from children, from the works of man, from the past, the present, the future and the unknown. I caused Him to be from fear and despair. I gathered in everything from this mighty act, all I have known, seen and experienced. My sin, my presumption, my vanity, my love, my hate, my lust. And last I gave myself and so made God. And He was magnificent. For He is all these things.

I was utterly in His presence. I knelt by the road. I took out the bread and the wine. Panem vinum in salutis consecramus hostiam. And in this understanding He gave Himself humbly and faithfully to me, as I had given myself to Him.

Silence.

SEWERMAN: You've found peace.

GRANDIER: More. I've found meaning.

SEWERMAN: That makes me happy.

GRANDIER: And, my son, I have found reason.

SEWERMAN: And that is sanity.

GRANDIER: I must go now. I must go to worship Him in His house, adore Him in His shrine. I must go to church.

GRANDIER *moves forward and enters the church.*

SOLDIERS *lounge against the altar.* DE LAUBARDEMONT *comes forward.*

LAUBARDEMONT: You are forbidden this place.

GRANDIER: Forbidden?

LAUBARDEMONT: You are an impious and libertine priest. You must not enter.

GRANDIER: It is my church! My beloved church!

LAUBARDEMONT: No longer. You're under arrest. Charges will be read. Come with me. Bring him.

GRANDIER, *between soldiers, is brought from the church into the sunlight,* DE LAUBARDEMONT *leading the way. They pass through the street.*

ADAM, MANNOURY *and* TRINCANT *lean from an upper window, jeering.*

PHILLIPE TRINCANT, *with a silent old man beside her, watches.*

RANGIER *and* MIGNON *move in the church with a censer, intoning, exorcising.*

BARRÉ *is on his knees in the street as* GRANDIER *passes.*

THE SEWERMAN *watches. A crowd of townspeople gather round him, noisy and enquiring.*

And as GRANDIER *moves on the street and the church are filled with the clamour and laughter of devils, issuing from every mouth.*

Laughter. Laughter.

CURTAIN

III

Night.

A cell. Another room above. GRANDIER *alone.*

Distant shouts and laughter from an unseen crowd.

BONTEMPS, *a gaoler, comes to Grandier.*

BONTEMPS: Have you slept?

GRANDIER: No. No, the noise. The crowd. Have they slept?

BONTEMPS: Thirty thousand people have come into the town. Where do you expect them to find beds?

GRANDIER: Why should they want to sleep, anyway? Did I, as a child, the night before the treat?

BONTEMPS: They're certainly looking forward to it.

GRANDIER: What? Say it.

BONTEMPS: The execution.

GRANDIER: I haven't been tried yet.

BONTEMPS: All right. Have it your own way. The trial, then.

GRANDIER: Are you a merciful man?

BONTEMPS: Look, this is your system. Just be thankful that you can get men to do the job. Don't ask that they should be humane as well. I came to tell you that you're to be called early. So try and get some sleep.

GRANDIER: Thank you.

BONTEMPS: Is there anything you want? There's not much I can offer.

GRANDIER: Nothing. Nothing.

JEANNE *and* FATHER MIGNON.

JEANNE: Don't go!

MIGNON: It's three o'clock in the morning. I'm an old man. Need sleep.

JEANNE: I don't want to be left alone with him.

MIGNON: With your persecutor? Grandier?

JEANNE: Yes.

MIGNON: He's under close guard.

JEANNE: No. He's here. Within me. Like a child. He never revealed to me what sort of man he was. I knew him to be beautiful. Many said he was clever, and many said he was wicked. But for all his violence to my soul and body he never came to me in anything but love. No, let me speak. He's within me, I say. I'm possessed. But he is still, lying beneath my heart, living through my breath and my blood. And he makes me afraid. Afraid that I may have fallen into the gravest error in this matter.

MIGNON: What do you mean?

JEANNE: Have I been mistaken? Did Satan take on the person of my love, my darling, so as to delude me?

MIGNON: Never. The man is his agent.

JEANNE: I have such a little body. It is a small battleground in which to decide this terrible struggle between good and evil, between love and hate. Was I wrong to allow it?

MIGNON: No, no. Don't you understand? These very thoughts are' put in your mind by the forces of dread. It's wrong to believe that Hell always fights with the clamour of arms. It is now, in the small hours, that Satan sends his secret agents, whispering, with their messages of doubt.

JEANNE: I don't know. I don't know. You all speak with so many voices. And I am very tired. (*she cries out*) Father! Father!

GRANDIER *alone in his cell*.

GRANDIER: There will be pain. It will kill God. My fear is driving Him out already.

Yes. Yes. We are flies upon the wall. Buzzing in the heat. That's so. That's so. No, no. We're monsters made up in a day. Clay in a baby's hands. Horrible, we should be bottled and hung in the pharmacy. Curiosities, for amusement only.

So. Nothing.

Shall I withstand the pain? Mother, mother, remember my fear!

Oh, nothing. This morning on the road. What was that? It was a little delusion of meaning. A trick of the sun, some fatigue of the body, and a man starts to believe that he's immortal. Look at me now. Wringing my hands, trying to convince myself that this flesh and bone is meaningful.

Sad, sad, though, very sad. To make a man see in the morning what the glory might be, and by night to snatch it from him.

Most Heavenly Father, though I struggle in Your arms like a fretful child —

This need to create a meaning. What arrogance it is! Expendable, that's what we are. Nothing proceeding to nothing.

Let me look into this void. Let me look into myself. Is there one thing, past or present, which makes for a purpose? (*silence*) Nothing. Nothing.

Who's there?

FATHER AMBROSE, *an old man, has come in.*

AMBROSE: My name is Ambrose.

GRANDIER: I know you, Father.

AMBROSE: I was told of your trouble, my son. The night can be very long.

GRANDIER: Yes. Stay with me.

AMBROSE: I thought I might read to you. Or, if you'd like it better, we can pray together.

GRANDIER: No. Help me.

AMBROSE: Let me try.

GRANDIER: They are destroying my faith. By fear and loneliness now. Later, by pain.

AMBROSE: Go to God, my son.

GRANDIER: Nothing going to nothing.

AMBROSE: God is here, and Christ is now.

GRANDIER: Yes. That is my faith. But how can I defend it?

AMBROSE: By remembering the will of God.

GRANDIER: Yes. Yes.

AMBROSE: By remembering that nothing must be asked of him, and nothing refused.

GRANDIER: Yes. But this is all in the books. I've read them, and understood them. And it is not enough. Not enough. Not now.

AMBROSE: God is here, and Christ is here.

GRANDIER: You're an old man. Have you gathered no more than this fustian in all your years? I'm sorry. You came in pure charity. The only one who has done so. I'm sorry.

AMBROSE *opens a book.*

AMBROSE: Suffering must be willed, affliction must be willed, humiliation must be willed, and in the act of willing —

GRANDIER: They'll be understood. I know. I know.

AMBROSE: Then you know everything.

GRANDIER: I know nothing. Speak to me as a man, Father. Talk about simple things.

AMBROSE: I came to help you, my son.

GRANDIER: You can help me. By speaking as a man. So shut your books. Forget other men's words. Speak to me.

AMBROSE: Ah, you believe there is some secret in simplicity. I am a simple man, it's true. I've never had any great doubt. Plain and shy, I have been less tempted than others, of course. The devil likes more magnificence than I've ever been able to offer. A peasant boy who clung to the love of God because he was too awkward to ask for the love of man.   I'm not a good example, my son. That's why I brought the books.

GRANDIER: You think too little of yourself.   What must we give God?

AMBROSE: Ourselves.

GRANDIER: But I am unworthy.

AMBROSE: Have you greatly sinned?

GRANDIER: Greatly.

AMBROSE: Even young girls come to me nowadays and confess things I don't know about.   So it's hardly likely that I'll understand the sins of a young man of the world such as you.   But let me try.

GRANDIER: There have been women and lust: power and ambition: worldliness and mockery.

AMBROSE: Remember.   God is here.   You speak before Him.   Christ is now.   You suffer with Him.

GRANDIER: I dread the pain to come.   The humiliation.

AMBROSE: Did you dread the ecstasy of love?

GRANDIER: No.

AMBROSE: Or its humiliation?

GRANDIER: I gloried in it.   I have lived by the senses.

AMBROSE: Then die by them.

GRANDIER: What did you say?

AMBROSE: Offer God pain, convulsion and disgust.

GRANDIER: Yes.   Give Him myself.

AMBROSE: Let Him reveal Himself in the only way you can understand.

GRANDIER: Yes! Yes!

AMBROSE: It is all any of us can do. We live a little while, and in that little while we sin. We go to Him as we can. All is forgiven.

GRANDIER: Yes. I am His child. It is true. Let Him take me as I am. So there is meaning. There is meaning, after all. I am a sinful man and I can be accepted. It is not nothing going to nothing. It is sin going to forgiveness. It is a human creature going to love.

BONTEMPS *has come in.*

BONTEMPS: He's got to leave. If you want a priest they say you can ask for Father Barré or Father Rangier.

GRANDIER: They say?

BONTEMPS: Out there.

GRANDIER: De Laubardemont?

BONTEMPS: That's right.

AMBROSE: Must I go? Does he say I must go?

GRANDIER: Yes, Father. You are dangerous in your innocence. But they are too late.

AMBROSE: I don't understand.

GRANDIER: It is better that way. Let me kiss you.

BONTEMPS *and* FATHER AMBROSE *go.*

GRANDIER *alone.*

GRANDIER: What? Tears? When was the last time this happened? What are they for? They must be for what is lost, not for what has been found.

For God is here.

Sudden daylight. Laughter.

CLAIRE, GABRIELLE *and* LOUISE *come into the open air.*

GABRIELLE: The town's like a fairground.

CLAIRE: They were singing not far from my window all night.

GABRIELLE: There are acrobats. I wish we could see them. I loved acrobats.

CLAIRE: Haven't we entertained each other enough in that way?

They laugh.

LOUISE: We don't seem to amuse other people any more. None of the Fathers or the great Parisians have been near us for days.

JEANNE *has come up to them, unobserved.*

JEANNE: You must understand, Louise, that the darlings of the public have their day, which ends, like any other.

LOUISE: Is it all over, Mother?

JEANNE: Soon. He's appearing before his judges this morning to make his last statement.

LOUISE: I didn't mean Father Grandier. I meant us. What shall we —

JEANNE: Then they'll speak the sentence. And at last there will be the Question.

LOUISE: But what will become of us, Mother?

JEANNE: We shall live. You've a lifetime before you, pretty Louise. Think of that.

A cell: MANNOURY *alone.*

ADAM *is let in.*

ADAM: Hullo.

MANNOURY: Hullo.

ADAM: Were you sent for?

MANNOURY: Yes.

ADAM: So was I. By De Laubardemont?

MANNOURY: That's it.

ADAM: I've brought my things. Have you?

MANNOURY: Yes.

ADAM: What I thought would be necessary.

MANNOURY: Difficult to say, isn't it?

ADAM: Have you done this before?

MANNOURY: No.

ADAM: Neither have I. Hm. Cold in here.

MANNOURY: Yes.

ADAM: Cold out.

MANNOURY: 'Tis.

ADAM: For a summer day.

MANNOURY: August. Yes.

DE LAUBARDEMONT *comes in.*

LAUBARDEMONT: Good morning, gentlemen. Glad to find you here. He's being brought back from the court. Should be on his way now.

MANNOURY: What exactly do you want us to do?

LAUBARDEMONT: Prepare the man. A decision has been reached. Unanimously. He is condemned.

ADAM: Well, well.

MANNOURY: Not surprising.

ADAM: There it is.

LAUBARDEMONT: I want you to be as quick as you can. There was an extraordinary amount of sympathy for the creature when he made his statement. There were even some unhealthy tears. So I want him ready and back there to hear the sentence as soon as possible.

MANNOURY: We'll do our best.

LAUBARDEMONT: Adam, would you be good enough to go and see the gaoler? He's getting all the necessary stuff together. Bring it in when he's done.

ADAM: All right.

ADAM *goes.*

LAUBARDEMONT: The man made something of an impression. Father Barré explained that it was the devil's doing. He said the calm was the brazen insolence of hell, and the dignity nothing but unrepentant pride. Still the man made quite an impression.

GRANDIER *is brought in by a Captain of the Guard. Grandier is dressed in full canonicals, looking his finest.*

GRANDIER: Good morning, Mister Surgeon.

MANNOURY: And good morning to you.

GRANDIER: De Laubardemont I've already seen.

LAUBARDEMONT: You must return to the court at once.

GRANDIER: Very well.

LAUBARDEMONT: For the sentence.

GRANDIER: I understand.

LAUBARDEMONT: So now I must ask you to undress.

GRANDIER: Undress?

LAUBARDEMONT: You can't go like that.

GRANDIER: I suppose not.

GRANDIER *takes off his biretta, and then begins to remove his cape.*

ADAM *comes in with* BONTEMPS. ADAM *carries a tray, on which there is a bowl of water, some oil and a razor.*

GRANDIER: Good morning, Mister Chemist. What have you got there?

ADAM (*stammering*): It's a razor.

GRANDIER (*after a moment: to De Laubardemont*): Must it be this way?

LAUBARDEMONT: Yes. Order of the court.

MANNOURY *has taken the razor: tests it on his thumb.*

GRANDIER: Well, Mister Surgeon, all your study and training have brought you only to this. Those late nights spent discussing the existence of existence have brought you only here. To be a barber.

LAUBARDEMONT: Get on with it.

GRANDIER: Just a moment.

GRANDIER *touches his black curls, and then fingers his moustaches.*

GRANDIER: Have you a glass?

LAUBARDEMONT: No, no. Of course not.

BONTEMPS: There's this.

BONTEMPS *takes an empty metal cup from the tray. He polishes the base of the cup on his sleeve and gives it to* GRANDIER.

GRANDIER *stands looking long and deeply at his reflection.*

A public place.

A large crowd. Town and country people. Yawning, at ease, calling to each other. Apart: an enclosure holding some well-dressed women of the bourgeoisie. Chatter from them. There is a clerk within a mountain of books.

Sudden silence. All heads turn towards us.

THE CLERK *rises. He reads:*

CLERK: Urbain Grandier, you have been found guilty of commerce with the devil. And that you used this unholy alliance to possess, seduce and debauch certain Sisters of the holy order of Saint Ursula (they are fully named in this document). You have also been found guilty of obscenity, blasphemy and sacrilege.

It is ordered that you proceed and kneel at the doors of Saint Peter's and Saint Ursula's and there, with a rope round your neck and a two pound taper in your hand, ask pardon of God, the King and Justice. Next, it is ordered that you be taken to the Place Sainte-Croix, tied to a stake and burned alive: after which your ashes will be scattered to the four winds.

It has been decided that a commemorative plaque shall be set up in the Ursulines' chapel. The cost of this, yet to be ascertained, will be chargeable to your confiscated estate.

Lastly, before sentence is carried out, you will be subjected to the Question, both ordinary and extraordinary.

Pronounced at Loudun, 18th August 1634, and executed the same day.

GRANDIER *slowly comes into sight. His hands are tied behind his back. He is dressed in a nightgown and slippers, but with a skull cap and biretta on his head.* DE LAUBARDEMONT, MANNOURY *and* ADAM *accompany him. Also* BARRÉ, RANGIER *and* MIGNON, *who are scattering holy water with consecrated whisks and intoning formulas of exorcism.*

DE LAUBARDEMONT *steps forward. He snatches the hat and cap from Grandier's head, and flings them to the ground.* GRANDIER *is revealed. He is completely shaven. Gone are the magnificent curls, the moustaches, even the eyebrows. He stands, a bald fool.*

There is a sudden, hysterical giggle from the women in the enclosure.

Silence.

GRANDIER *speaks to us.*

GRANDIER: My lords, I call God the Father, God the Son, and God the Holy Ghost, together with the Virgin, to witness that I have never been a sorcerer. The only magic I have practised is that of the Holy Scripture. I am innocent.

Silence. Then murmurs from the women: a silly laugh.

I am innocent, and I am afraid. I fear for my salvation. I am prepared to go and meet God, but the horrible
torment you have ordered for me on the way may drive
my wretched soul to despair. Despair, my lords. It is the
gravest of sins. It is the short way to eternal damnation.
Surely in your wisdom you do not mean to kill a soul.
So may I ask you, in your mercy, to mitigate, if only a
little, my punishment.

GRANDIER *looks from face to face: silence.*

Very well. When I was a child I was told about the
martyrs. I loved the men and women who died for the
honour of Jesus Christ. In a time of loneliness I have
often wished to be of their company. Now, foolish and
obscure priest that I am, I cannot presume to place
myself among these great and holy men. But may I say
that I have the hope in my heart that as this day ends
Almighty God, my beloved Father in Heaven, will glance
aside and let my suffering atone for my vain and disordered life. Amen.

*Silence. Then somewhere in the crowd a man's voice clearly
echoes Grandier's amen. Then another. Silence again. Only
the sound of a woman bitterly weeping.*

DE LAUBARDEMONT *to the Captain of the Guard:*

LAUBARDEMONT: Get them all out of here!

*At once the guards began to clear the place. The public go away
along corridors and down steps, complaining, some protesting.*

GRANDIER *is left with* DE LAUBARDEMONT, *the* CLERK,
BARRÉ, RANGIER *and* MIGNON. *He has not moved, as he
stands facing his judges.*

DE CERISAY *and* D'ARMAGNAC *can be seen. They are apart,
overlooking the scene.*

DE LAUBARDEMONT *faces Grandier: speaks to him.*

LAUBARDEMONT: Confess your guilt. Tell us the names of your accomplices. Then perhaps my lords, the judges, will consider your appeal.

GRANDIER: I cannot name accomplices I've never had, nor confess to crimes I've not done.

LAUBARDEMONT: This attitude will do you no good. You will suffer for it.

GRANDIER: I know that. And I am proud.

LAUBARDEMONT: Proud, sir? That word does not become your situation. Now look here, my dear fellow—untie his hands—this document is a simple confession. Here is a pen. Just put your name to this paper and we can forget the next stage of the proceedings.

GRANDIER: You must excuse me. No.

LAUBARDEMONT: I just want your signature. Here. That's all.

GRANDIER: My conscience forbids me to put my name to something which is untrue.

LAUBARDEMONT: You'll save us all a lot of trouble if you'll sign. The document being true, of course. (*he shouts*) True! You've been found guilty.

GRANDIER: I'm sorry.

LAUBARDEMONT: I fear for you, Grandier. I fear for you very much. I have seen men before you take this brave standing in the shadow of the Question. It was unwise, Grandier. Think again.

GRANDIER: No.

LAUBARDEMONT: You will go into the darkness before your death. Let me talk to you for a moment about pain. It is very difficult for us standing here, both healthy men, to imagine the shattering effect of agony. The sun's warm on your face at the moment, isn't it? And you can curl your toes if you want in your slippers. You are alive, and you know it. But when you are stretched out in that little room, with the pain screaming through you like a voice, let me tell you what you will think. First: how can man do this to man? Then: how can God allow it? Then: there can be no God. Then: there is no God. The voice of pain will grow stronger, and your resolution weaker. Despair, Grandier. You used the word yourself. You called it the gravest sin. Don't reject God at this moment. Reconcile yourself. For you have bitterly offended Him. Confess.

GRANDIER: No.

D'ARMAGNAC: Are those tears on De Laubardemont's face?

DE CERISAY: I'm afraid so.

D'ARMAGNAC: Does he believe what he's saying?

DE CERISAY: Yes. Touching, isn't it?

LAUBARDEMONT (*to Grandier*): Very well. I ask you once more. Once more! Will you sign?

GRANDIER *shakes his head.*

LAUBARDEMONT: Take him away.

The guard surrounds Grandier.

GRANDIER: I would like to ask something.

LAUBARDEMONT: What?

GRANDIER: May I have Father Ambrose with me?

LAUBARDEMONT: No.

GRANDIER: He's a harmless old man. He won't impede you.

LAUBARDEMONT: He's no longer in the town. He's been sent away. If you want spiritual consolation address yourself to one of these gentlemen.

GRANDIER *stares at Barré, Rangier and Mignon for a moment before turning away between the guards and going.* DE LAUBARDEMONT *and the* CLERK *follow.*

MIGNON: I found the Commissioner's last appeal very moving.

RANGIER: Very.

BARRÉ: I suppose you understand that Grandier's refusal to sign was the final proof of guilt.

MIGNON: Yes. Yes, I suppose so.

BARRÉ: Lucifer has sealed his mouth: hardened his heart against repentance.

MIGNON: Of course. That's the reason.

BARRÉ: Shall we go?

BARRÉ, RANGIER *and* MIGNON *go.*

D'ARMAGNAC: Come to my house with me, De Cerisay.

DE CERISAY: All right, sir.

D'ARMAGNAC: I don't want you to talk to me.

DE CERISAY: Very well.

D'ARMAGNAC: We'll just sit together. And think over the day. Two—I hope—reasonable men. We'll sit and—

we'll drink. Yes, that's it, we'll get drunk. Drunk
enough to see visions. Come on.

D'ARMAGNAC *and* DE CERISAY *go.*

A garden. JEANNE *enters. She is bare-headed, and dressed only
in a simple white under-garment. Her little, deformed person
looks childlike. She has a rope round her neck, and carries a
candle in her hand. She stands quite still.*

CLAIRE, GABRIELLE *and* LOUISE *gather some little way from*
JEANNE, *frightened, watching her.* Then CLAIRE *comes
forward to her.*

CLAIRE: Come in, dear Mother.

JEANNE: No, child.

CLAIRE: But the sun is very hot after the rain. It will
do you no good.

JEANNE: Find me a place—it needn't be so high—where
I can tie this rope. I have been looking.

CLAIRE: No, Mother. It is the most terrible sin.

JEANNE: Sin?

CLAIRE: Yes.

CLAIRE *unknots the rope and takes it away.* LOUISE *comes
forward with a cloak, which she puts about Jeanne.*

LOUISE: Don't frighten us, Mother.

JEANNE: I have been woken night after night by the sound
of weeping. I've gone about trying to find out who it is.
I have a heart like anyone else. It can be broken by such
a sound.

LOUISE: It's no one here.

JEANNE: I'd never have thought it was possible for anyone to suffer such despair, such desolation.

LOUISE: But it's no one.

JEANNE: No one?

CLAIRE: It is the devil. He can snivel to order. Yes, Mother, think. Father Grandier would have you go to hell with him. So he gets the devil to cry at night and break your heart, makes you put a rope round your neck, and hang yourself. Don't be deceived.

JEANNE: Is there no way? And is that Claire speaking? Claire, who used to talk to me of the innocence of Christ? What's the time?

LOUISE: Just past noon.

JEANNE: Let me sit here. I promise not to harm myself. Leave me.

CLAIRE, LOUISE *and* GABRIELLE *go, leaving* JEANNE *alone.*

The silence is broken by a hideous sound of hammering. A scream.

The upper room. GRANDIER *is stretched on the floor, bound. His legs, from the knees to the feet, are enclosed in a kind of box. Movable boards within the box, driven inward by huge wedges, crush his legs.* BONTEMPS *is hammering the wedges home.*

MANNOURY, ADAM *and* MIGNON *are crouched in the lower room.*

BARRÉ, *who is sitting by Grandier's head, leans forward.*

BARRÉ: Will you confess?

Slowly, GRANDIER *shakes his head.* BARRÉ *glances at* DE LAUBARDEMONT, *who stands against the wall.*

LAUBARDEMONT (*to Bontemps*): Another.

BONTEMPS *picks up another wedge, but it is at once snatched out of his hand by* RANGIER.

RANGIER: Just a moment! (*he sprinkles the wedge with holy water, and makes signs over it*) Very necessary. The devil has the power, you see, to make the pain less than it should be.

BONTEMPS: Finished?

RANGIER: Yes.

He gives the wedge to BONTEMPS, *who inserts it.*

BARRÉ: Hit! Hit!

BOTEMPS *strikes with the mallet. A scream.*

In the lower room.

MANNOURY: What's the cubic capacity of a man's breath?

ADAM: Don't know.

MANNOURY: Just wondered.

ADAM: It doesn't occur to you when you start something, that—Hm.

MANNOURY: What did you say?

ADAM: Nothing. Just thinking aloud.

A blow with the mallet. BARRÉ *leans forward.*

BARRÉ: Confess.

GRANDIER: I'm only too ready to confess my real sins. I have been a man, I have loved women. I have been proud. I have longed for power.

BARRÉ: That's not what we want. You've been a magician. You've had commerce with devils.

GRANDIER: No. No.

BARRÉ: Another. Oh, give it to me!

BARRÉ *snatches the wedge and the mallet from* BONTEMPS *and, with the wedge unexorcised, drives it home with two mighty blows.*

GRANDIER'S *scream echoes in the garden where* JEANNE *sits alone.*

JEANNE: Is it only in the very depths that one finds God? Look at me. First I wanted to come to Him in innocence. It was not enough. Then there was the lying and play-acting. The guilt, the humiliation. It was not enough. There were the antics done for the dirty eyes of priests. The squalor. It was not enough. Down, down further.

The sound of hammering. GRANDIER'S *voice:*

GRANDIER: God. God. God. Don't abandon me. Don't let this pain make me forget You.

JEANNE: Down. Down. Into idiot oblivion. No thought. No feeling. Nothing. Is God here?

The upper room. DE LAUBARDEMONT *comes forward.*

LAUBARDEMONT: Take him out. It's no good.

BARRÉ, RANGIER *and* BONTEMPS *lift* GRANDIER *from the box and seat him on a stool.* BONTEMPS *covers Grandier's shattered legs with a rug.* GRANDIER *stares down at himself.*

GRANDIER: Attendite et videte si est dolor sicut dolor meus.

JEANNE *gets up.*

JEANNE: Where are You? Where are You?

JEANNE *goes from the garden.*

BARRÉ *and* RANGIER *have come down into the lower room.*

ADAM: Any good?

BARRÉ: No.

MANNOURY: No confession?

BARRÉ: No.

ADAM: I say!

BARRÉ: Perfectly good reason.

MANNOURY: What?

BARRÉ: He called on God to give him strength. His god is the devil and did so. Made him insensible to pain. We'll get nowhere like this.

ADAM: Insensible to pain? What were all those screams?

BARRÉ: A mockery

BARRÉ, MIGNON *and* RANGIER *go down into the street.*

The upper room.

GRANDIER: Take no notice of these tears. They're only weakness.

LAUBARDEMONT: Remorse?

GRANDIER: No.

LAUBARDEMONT: Confess.

GRANDIER: No. There are two things a man should never be asked to do in front of other men. Perform with a

woman, and suffer pain. You people know how to bring
hell on earth for someone like me. Make it all public.

LAUBARDEMONT: That is vanity, Father.

GRANDIER: Is it? I don't think so. A man is a private
thing. He belongs to himself. Those two most intimate
experiences, love and pain, have nothing to do with the
mob. How can they concern it? For the mob can feel
neither.

LAUBARDEMONT: The mob is made up of Christian souls.
Six thousand of them are waiting for you in the market
place. Tell me, do you love the Church?

GRANDIER: With all my heart.

LAUBARDEMONT: Do you want to see it grow more powerful, more benevolent, until it embraces every human
soul on this earth?

GRANDIER: That would be my wish.

LAUBARDEMONT: Then help us to achieve this great
purpose. Go to the market place a penitent man.
Confess, and by confessing, proclaim to these thousands
that you have returned to the Church's arms. By going
to the stake unrepentant you do God a disservice. You
give hope to the sceptics and unbelievers. You make
them glad. Such an act can mine the very foundations
of the Church. Think. You are no longer important.
Are you any longer important?

GRANDIER: No.

LAUBARDEMONT: Then make a last supreme gesture for
the Catholic faith.

Silence. DE LAUBARDEMONT *eagerly leans forward. Then*
GRANDIER *looks up. His face is drawn in an agonized smile.*

GRANDIER: This is sophistry, Laubardemont, and you're too intelligent not to know it. Pay me the same compliment.

LAUBARDEMONT: You can laugh? Now?

GRANDIER: Yes. Because I know more about it than you.

LAUBARDEMONT: When I tell you, Grandier—

GRANDIER: Don't persist. I can destroy you. At least in argument. Keep you illusions, Mister Commissioner. You'll need them all to deal with the men who will come after me.

LAUBARDEMONT: Confess.

GRANDIER: No.

LAUBARDEMONT: Confess.

GRANDIER: No.

LAUBARDEMONT: Sign.

GRANDIER: No.

DE LAUBARDEMONT *goes to the door. He calls down the stairs.*

LAUBARDEMONT: Let me have the guard here!

A street.

A crowd is staring into the distance. The people are quiet, shifting, uneasy, withheld. BARRÉ, RANGIER *and* MIGNON *come towards them.* RANGIER *and* MIGNON *are scattering holy water and intoning exorcisms.* BARRÉ *moves along the crowd, taking men and women by the arm, speaking to them individually.*

BARRÉ: My dear children, you are about to witness the passage of a wicked and unrepentant man to hell. I beg of you—you, sir—take the sight to your heart. Let it be a lesson that will stay with you—my good woman—all your life. Watch this infamous magician who has trafficked with devils and ask yourself—my child—is this what a man comes to when he scorns God?

A drum. GRANDIER *comes into sight. He is seated on a chair which has been lashed to a kind of litter, and is carried by four soldiers. He wears a shirt impregnated with sulphur, a vivid yellow, and there is a rope round his neck. His broken legs dangle. He is a ridiculous, hairless, shattered doll.* THE CLERK *walks beside him.* DE LAUBARDEMONT *and soldiers follow.*

Saint Ursula's Convent.

The procession comes to the convent door and stops. THE CLERK *puts a two pound taper into Grandier's hand.*

LAUBARDEMONT: You must get down here.

GRANDIER: What is this place?

LAUBARDEMONT: It is the Convent of Saint Ursula. A place you have defiled.

A SOLDIER *lifts* GRANDIER *from the litter like a child, and puts him on the ground.*

LAUBARDEMONT: Do what must be done.

GRANDIER: In this strange and unknown place I ask pardon of God, the King and Justice. I beg that I may— (*he falls forward on his face: cries out*) Deus meus, miserere mei Deus!

The convent door opens and from the dark entrance come JEANNE, GABRIELLE, CLAIRE *and* LOUISE.

LAUBARDEMONT: Ask pardon of this Prioress, and these good Sisters.

GRANDIER: Who are these women?

LAUBARDEMONT: They are the people you have wronged. Ask their forgiveness.

GRANDIER: I have done no such thing. I can only ask that God will forgive them.

Utter silence as GRANDIER *and* JEANNE *stare at each other.*

JEANNE: They always spoke of your beauty. Now I see it with my own eyes and I know it to be true.

GRANDIER: Look at this thing which I am, and learn the meaning of love.

The drum. GRANDIER *is lifted back on to the litter. The procession moves on into the distance.*

A great bell. Voices:

Dies irae, dies illa, solvet saeclum in favilla, teste David cum Sybilla.

Quantus tremor est futurus, quando judex est venturus, cuncta stricte discussurus!

JEANNE, *alone, comes forward. Darkness.*

The streets of Loudun. Night.

The town seems to be on fire. Distant buildings are silhouetted against a harsh red sky. A church door gapes like a sulphurous mouth.   Armed men with banners cross a bridge.   A man is climbing a ladder, waving into the distance in hopeless distress.

The crowd (which watched Grandier into the distance) has broken up and is rushing, hysterical, screaming, laughing, through the streets.

JEANNE *wanders on alone.*

MANNOURY *and* ADAM.

MANNOURY: Very odd, you know.

ADAM: What?

MANNOURY: That business of human fat being rendered down by heat to the consistency of candle wax and then igniting with a flame of such exquisite colour.

ADAM: Rum business, altogether.

MANNOURY: Interesting, though.   I'd say, Adam, if there's any aesthetic appeal in your work as a chemist it lies in that direction.   Wouldn't you?

ADAM: Maybe.

They go.

BARRÉ, MIGNON *and* RANGIER.

BARRÉ: He's in hell.   Be sure of it.

MIGNON: Tonight he roasts.

BARRÉ: Unrepentant, frightful man!

RANGIER: You know, I saw his women sitting there, watching.   One was in tears, it's true.   But she was watching.   Never turned away.

BARRÉ: Devils.   All devils.   What's the matter with you?

MIGNON: I don't feel very well.

BARRÉ (*hitting him on the back*): Smoke got down you, I expect.

MIGNON: I think I'll go to bed now, if you don't mind.

BARRÉ: We're all going to get to our beds, Mignon. How long we shall be allowed to lie there depends on friend Satan. We vanquished him and brought peace to this place today. But you can be sure that even now he is creeping back. Ah, my dear friends, men of our kind will never lack employment.

They go.

PHILLIPE TRINCANT. *She is monstrously pregnant, and lumbers forward leading the* OLD MAN *by the hand.*

PHILLIPE: Come along home, dear husband. You must try to walk a little quicker. What? (*the* OLD MAN *whispers to her*) Watching all this today has made you quite excited. (*he whispers again*) Yes, you shall do whatever you like. And I'll do all I can for you. Wipe your mouth. We've many happy years ahead together. What? Yes, of course there's a way. I'll turn and turn about for you. Jesus, I will. I'll show you tricks. So come home, darling.

PHILLIPE *and the* OLD MAN *go.*

D'ARMAGNAC *and* DE CERISAY. *They are drunk.*

D'ARMAGNAC: We shouldn't be doing this, De Cerisay. We are the rational, forward looking men of our age. We should be taking a stand.

DE CERISAY: Quite right.

D'ARMAGNAC: About something or other. I'm not quite sure what. Why is the air full of insects tonight? What was I saying?

DE CERISAY: We should take a stand.

D'ARMAGNAC: And assert ourselves.

DE CERISAY: What about?

D'ARMAGNAC: What we believe.

DE CERISAY: And what do we believe?

D'ARMAGNAC: Ask me tomorrow. Am I mad? Were they fornicating in the street up there? And what did that old woman have in the basket? Human remains? Why was that animal leading a man on a rope? What is the strange, sweet smell that hangs over the place? And that musician crucified upon the harp. What does it all mean, De Cerisay? As rational men we should be able to explain it.

DE CERISAY: I can't.

D'ARMAGNAC: Neither can I. So take me home.

They go.

JEANNE's *wandering through the streets has brought her to the* SEWERMAN.

SEWERMAN: When it was done they shovelled him to the north, the south, the east and the west.

JEANNE: Do you know who I am?

SEWERMAN: Yes, madam, I know.

Some of the crowd are passing. They are fighting among themselves for some objects which are passed from hand to hand.

JEANNE: What are they doing?

SEWERMAN: It's bits of the body they're after.

JEANNE: As relics?

SEWERMAN: Don't try to comfort yourself. No, they want them as charms. There's a difference, you know. (*he snatches a charred bone from one of the men*) They don't want to adore this. They want it to cure their constipation or their headache, to have it bring back their virility or their wife. They want it for love or hate. (*he holds out the bone*) Do you want it for anything?

JEANNE *shakes her head. The crowd has gone.* THE SEWERMAN *goes.*

JEANNE *alone. She cries out in her own voice:*

JEANNE: Grandier! Grandier!

Silence.

CURTAIN